THE COMPLETE GUIDE TO RETIREMENT

THE COMPLETE GUIDE TO RETIREMENT

THOMAS COLLINS

PRENTICE-HALL, INC.
Englewood Cliffs, N.J.

To
BEULAH
who is too young to read it

PREFACE

The author has been traveling down the annuity alleys of America for the last twenty years, talking to people who have retired. He is currently receiving around two thousand letters a month from those who read his syndicated retirement columns across the country.

Out of all this, he has written this book.

He has written it in the language of the people. He has put it in the context—the humor, the savvy, the needs—of those who have lived through four major American wars, income taxes, bathtub gin, and children and have now come up to retirement in this second half of the century.

THOMAS COLLINS

CONTENTS

CONTENTS

PRELUDE

A RETIREMENT PRAYER

If I were a member of the retirement set or were about to join it, the man said, I think I would want to say a prayer. To Whomever I believed in. Or Whatever. Or maybe just to the sky.

The prayer would go something like this:

Grant me the integrity not to squander this precious freedom that comes to me with retirement. Man and woman have not had freedom with pay before. I have it. With the privilege to speak, to shout, to go, to come, to fight, to work, to dream, to do . . . without jeopardy to my pension or my freedom. I pray that I can comprehend what this unprecedented gift means. That I can use it to make a square foot of this world better.

Grant me the physical power—the hormones, the glands, the spirit, or whatever it is—to fight off the laziness that comes with freedom with pay . . . the narcotic of security.

Grant me the understanding to smile at the youngsters who move in to take over the job or career I have mastered so long. They know what they do . . . they work desperately for success and the money and glory it brings. So, no less, did I. Guide me to toleration of the indifference or scorn they have for one who went before them. Quiet my stomach as it rebels against the affronts to my dignity, my achievements, my efforts in my work that now seem to be cast aside.

Grant me the realization that goodness, if I am ever to achieve it, must come now. It is not later than I think. At age sixty-five I have still some potent years to be good. To discard the shadowy techniques I employed to mold my career and keep my job, to kill the striving at somebody else's cost, to end the envy, the jealousy, the distrust, the vanity, the bitterness, the hate. I pray that these ugly things which can give nothing to the power and glory of retirement be cast from me. And that I come at long last to be simply a good person.

Grant me the curiosity to investigate at this late time the great religions of the world. Surely there is more to them than the Medicine Man and the ritual, more than consolation from thunder and the mysteries of the Great Beyond, more than a swap of potted asphalt for Streets of Gold. What? Surely the religions that have served mankind so long have something more meaningful than all this, more important than being usher next Sunday or being elected to the board of deacons. What? Grant me the curiosity to find out.

Grant me, I implore you, the power to believe. In my retirement years it is not sufficient that I believe in the stability of the U.S. dollar, the survival of the insurance company that issues my pension check, and the price of cabbage at the grocery store. I need something more. And I would ask that I be able to walk out on my front porch of an afternoon when the sun is setting, to mull for a bit over the great issues of mankind, and say, as a fellow on radio once did, "This I Believe!"

Grant me what I have asked here and I cannot promise to paint a picture on the ceiling of a Sistine Chapel, or lie under a tomb in Westminster, or found a presidential library in an American small town. But I will do something. I will have the stuff to make a pay-back.

—from *The Golden Years* newspaper column

THE COMPLETE GUIDE TO RETIREMENT

~~~~~~~

ONE

PREPARING FOR RETIREMENT

There is a notion abroad in the land that it is a simple thing to retire: somebody tells you you've had it, somebody else gives you a party, then you pick up your hat and go.

This is not exactly the way it is.

To retire, if you do it properly, will perhaps be the largest operation of your lifetime. To marry was a matter of a license, a blood test, and a preacher. To get a job was a matter of filling out some forms. To go into the army was just learning to say "Yes, sir."

To retire is more complex. And while it is no ordeal—in fact, some people find adventure in it—it calls for a timetable and a checklist. It starts with the fellow you work for.

The Front Office

At least six months before retirement, but preferably a year, go to the person handling employee affairs and ask some questions. If it is a large company or institution you work for, the person will probably be the personnel officer. If a small one, it will be your boss. In either case you needn't be bashful about it because all employers have a tender heart for anybody about to retire, and in these days are most careful to be helpful.

You need from this person in the Front Office certain specific facts, and it will be well for you to take along a pencil and pad to record the answers you get. This would please the personnel officer. You could also take along your spouse if you're married. This would please him even more. He does not want you to have any misunderstandings about what you will get in retirement and why.

Your first question is about the pension. How much will it be? The personnel officer, after phoning your supervisor to see if you're not about to get a big raise or not about to be fired, can probably give you the exact figure a year before you retire. Write it down.

Next you want to know which of the fringe benefits you now have will carry over into retirement. What about the medical insurance? What about the life insurance? If you will continue to get them, will they cost you anything?

Ask what company or bank will send your pension and provide the other benefits, if any. Ask the address. Ask if this is where you complain if the pension or some other benefits don't arrive on time. (To the surprise of many retired people, their employer is usually completely divorced from the retirement payoff. Checks come in from strange companies in New York or Chicago.)

Now, when does the first pension check arrive? One month after retirement? On the first day of the month immediately following retirement? When?

If the life insurance remains in force, how much will it pay your survivors? In a lump sum? If any medical insurance is carried over, what will it pay—prior to age sixty-five and Medicare, and after age sixty-five?

This will pretty well take care of the business of money. Now for some nuts and bolts:

You will reach your retirement date—age sixty-two or sixty-five —on April 15. Do you retire that day? At the end of the month?

The half year? Or can you finish out the year? Is the choice up to you or the employer?

What about your accrued vacation time? If you go April 15, do you get a third of it? Or does the employer want to be generous and grant you your full two weeks? Also, can you elect to start the vacation on the day you retire and thus get cash for it, or can you include it in your retirement and leave two weeks early?

Taking cash instead of the vacation isn't a bad idea, since there's a long vacation in your future anyway. Including the vacation in your retirement isn't a good idea; you'll miss out on the retirement party and gift your co-workers, just maybe, are planning to give you.

One other item. If April 15 falls on a Wednesday, will you be paid only through Wednesday or for the full week? When do you get the check?

These are the essential questions you need answered in the Front Office. And don't worry that you have annoyed the personnel officer. Being helpful to employees is how he got his white shirt and fancy desk, and he probably wishes more employees would do what you have done.

With this in mind, you might at this point lay your pencil and pad aside, smile at the fellow, and ask if there is any retirement gravy that is not listed in the employee manual. Often there is. The employer, as an example, may have a couple of cubbyhole desks with typewriters that you can come in and use after you retire. There may be a tool shop in the basement that will be available to you. There may be a permanent invitation to the annual employee picnic. If the employer is a manufacturer and makes a consumer product, there may be a way you can get it wholesale. If the employer is a big one, there may be legal advice and counseling service you can tap. Most of these you'd never know about unless you asked. Now is the time to do it.

As a parting shot you can ask the personnel officer what your Social Security benefit will be. But it'll waste your time and his because he can give you only a guess. The only place you can pin down this information accurately is at a Social Security office. This should be your next stop.

3

Social Security

The Social Security office you visit should be the one nearest your home. Check the phone book, or ask at the post office. Your visit could be a year before retirement. It certainly shouldn't be less than four months.

On this first visit you want only information: to see if your account is in order, what the deadline is for application on both Social Security and Medicare, what documents you will need in making application.

You will find your reception at the office pleasant, with a clerk probably referring you to a desk behind a partition where somebody will answer your questions.

It is on your second visit, when you make your formal application, that the chips go down. You will have to produce your birth certificate or some other proof of age. If you are a husband, and if your wife has reached sixty-two, she can apply for Social Security at the same time you do. She will also need proof of age. And one of you had better have a marriage certificate to prove that you are really married.

The wife can wait until age sixty-five to start collecting benefits, which would be larger then, but whenever she elects to collect, the benefit becomes strictly hers. She will collect it for life, will get a raise if her husband dies, and can demand that her check be sent to her separately.

Most wives don't know this and become beholden to their husbands for the benevolent handout. The husband has nothing to do with it. She can thank the United States Congress.

From Social Security you should learn, as with your pension, on what date the checks will start, where you can complain if they don't arrive, and how you can get the checks regularly if you decide to retire to the South Pacific.

You should also pin down the sum you can expect on the Social Security check, what your death benefit will be, and if you are a husband just what monthly sum your wife will get if you die.

Your Correct Age

Your retirement date, your company benefits, your pension, your Social Security, are all based on how old you are. Do you really know? Or are you just presuming because somebody told you as a child what your age was? And, incidentally, have you been lying about it for the last thirty years?

On your age, retirement is the moment of truth. And what you think or what you claim isn't good enough. You must have proof. You can get it if your birth certificate was filed in the courthouse in the county where you were born. You can get it from United States census records by writing the Personal Census Service Branch, Bureau of the Census, Pittsburg, Kansas. A family Bible, old church records, or old military records may give you the proof you need.

If you have been lying, go back to the boss and to Social Security soon after your initial visits to them and lay your cards on the table.

Your Actual Retirement Income

Learning what your pension and Social Security will be is only the first step in determining what your retirement income will be. They will be gross figures, which may be about 30 percent of your salary. You want the net figure, which will show how rich or poor you are going to be, and this figure may be about 70 percent of the salary.

You get this net figure by adding up the costs of your job, which have been considerable. You start with your salary. Which isn't. Your take-home pay is your salary, no matter how much your vanity likes to claim the higher figure. So compute the take-home pay on a monthly basis (multiplying by fifty-two and dividing by twelve if you have been paid weekly). Since pension and Social Security will come to you monthly, you need the monthly figure to get an honest comparison. Put this monthly figure on a separate sheet of paper, then put beside it the total of what your pension and Social Security will be.

Now you get down to cases. On another sheet of paper start listing what you have been paying for the privilege of holding your job:

TAXES. While working you pay taxes on what your vanity says you make, not your take-home salary. In retirement you pay only on what you actually get, minus that part of your pension which you contributed. This would usually put you in a much lower tax bracket. In addition you get extra deductions when you reach age sixty-five.

TRANSPORTATION. This is a substantial figure if you ride a bus or train to work. It is a frightening one if you drive a car. You can add up the bus or train fares fairly easily. You'll have difficulty with the car costs, but if after all these years you'll stop kidding yourself, you can get a reasonable figure. Which will shock you.

LUNCHES. Unless you have been taking salami sandwiches to work in a pail, you have been spending at least $15 to $25 a month for lunches. In retirement you make your wife feed you free out of her budget, except that in retirement you lose your lunch appetite.

COFFEE BREAKS. Stop kidding yourself again. Would thirty cents a day cover it?

UNMENTIONABLES. The beers and bars so conveniently located between the job and home in the afternoon take several dollars a month out of a man's pocket. But your wife naturally knows you haven't been engaging in this sort of thing, so you might slip the bar costs into the Donations category.

DONATIONS. For baby gifts, wedding gifts, retirement parties, funeral flowers, pet charity drives of the boss, etc. These all stop at retirement. Theoretically, these wouldn't stop at retirement but actually they do. Partly because you're out of sight of the solicitors, and partly because, at 65, babies and weddings are out of vour generation orbit.

CLOTHES. White shirts, ties, decent shoes, a couple of good suits, socks, are all part of the costs of a job, along with a daily

6

shave and frequent haircuts. Most men and women never make a major clothes purchase after retirement.

DUES.   To professional groups, trade societies, labor unions, luncheon clubs.

BAD BETS.   On the Rose Bowl game, the Kentucky Derby, the World Series, prizefighters, and employee lottery pools.

Add all these costs of your job, plus $300 a year for the mad dash out of town on summer vacations (which you'll not be getting anymore). Subtract the figure you get from the take-home pay on your other sheet. Then compare with the retirement income.

You will see now what your actual, net retirement income will be. And it'll make you feel good for a month.

Thirty Days Hath September

You have probably been getting your salary weekly or twice monthly. You aren't going to get your retirement income that way. And you may be eating a lot of soup toward the end of the month unless you prepare in advance to change your spending budget to a monthly basis. Social Security checks and most pension checks arrive once a month, usually around the first.

You think it'll be simple to switch over? It won't.

Income Taxes

Double-check your income tax returns for the two years before retirement. Then pay up for any sins. You don't want tax men coming around with a $400 underpayment bill after you've gone on a pension.

Your Valuable Papers

Among your most invaluable possessions as you head into retirement are what are called your "valuable papers." A couple

7

of them you will need for the retirement process, such as proof of age for both man and wife and proof of marriage. The others, while usually not related to retirement, should be put in order as you prepare to retire.

The reason: If you don't do it now, you will pass up your last excuse, your last dramatic reminder, and will probably never do it. You will thus leave chaos to your survivors and may cost them a large part of your estate.

Your valuable papers, in addition to proof of age and marriage (three copies of each for future needs), will normally include the following:

> House deed, or apartment lease
> House insurance
> Life insurance policies
> Health insurance policies
> Car title and insurance
> Pension papers
> Military service records
> All stocks, bonds, and other certificates of investment, plus notations of all savings accounts
> Income tax returns for the last three years
> Copies of all contracts you hold
> List of debts, owed or due
> Name of bank holding your checking account
> The wills of you and your spouse

These papers should be placed in a safety deposit box at a bank or some other reliable institution, or in a disaster-proof container at home. The safety box is better, and you will probably be provided two keys to it.

One of these keys should be attached to a "Letter of Instructions" you will now write, making two copies of it. This letter will tell whom to notify in case of unexpected tragedy to you (husbands and wives often die in the same traffic accident or the same fire and sometimes die of simultaneous illnesses). The letter will also tell where your valuable papers are kept.

One copy of the letter should be kept in the home where it can be found readily. The other copy, with the second key to the safety box, should go outside the home—into the safe of your lawyer or into the hands of a trusted friend who will be around if anything happens to you.

This pretty well takes care of the valuable papers, but if you're feeling kindly there are a couple of additional matters regarding them that you might consider.

Put with the papers a document, witnessed by your lawyer, that gives your spouse power of attorney to sign your name. Sudden illness, an accident, or mental disability could tie up your incoming checks, your investments and bank accounts, leaving your spouse in a sorry state for ready cash.

Clean out from your papers, from your desk, or from dresser drawers all letters or papers that could be embarrassing or incriminating to anybody if discovered after your death. Retirement is a time to forgive.

Have You Hidden Any Cash?

As you prepare for retirement, you have reached that sad moment when you had better dig up the coins you have buried in the fruit jar at the back of the garage. And rescue the currency you have hidden between the joints of your house or under the basement floor.

You aren't going to die tomorrow, but there are people who die and leave behind some hidden treasure, never to be found by their survivors because they never told anybody about it.

Older people who themselves are hiding away some Kennedy half-dollars think older people wouldn't do this sort of thing. The reason they think so is because they seldom hear of any such cases. The reason they don't is because when some lucky person comes across the treasure, maybe twenty years later, the first thing he does is to keep his mouth shut. If you found $300 hidden in the attic of a home you bought fifteen years ago, would you advertise the fact? Most other people wouldn't either. And so, since the finding of hidden treasure seldom gets public notice, nobody really knows just how much has been found.

If you can't bring yourself to tell your spouse or a child where you've hidden something away, and if you can't bear to give up your hideaway game, then at least leave a sealed envelope somewhere among your valuable papers with a note telling what is hidden where. While you're about it you might also list any secret accounts you have set up in banks or savings and loan associations, which are also a weakness of older people. There is a bit more evidence available on these than on the more romantic hidden coins because savings institutions have to make reports of accounts whose owners have disappeared—usually into a cemetery—without a sliver of information left for the family about them.

Rediscovering Your Children

The eve of retirement is the time to start mending the family fences. Men, absorbed by their jobs and careers, tend to leave their children, along with the meter reader and the groceries, to their wives after age forty-five or so. The wife writes the letters, sends the Christmas gifts to the grandchildren, remembers the anniversaries.

Father steps in only when somebody wants some money, and then it is frequently to say "no." As a result, many fathers come up to age sixty-five as stern and shadowy creatures.

Men should start working to build a new image as they approach retirement because their children and grandchildren are likely in the end to be their greatest retirement blessing.

They need tact to do this. After all, it would hardly be manly for them to rush out and start writing letters to the children and remembering the birthdays and thus steal the glory from their wives who all these years have held things together. It would be like going home in retirement, getting lonely, and stealing the affections of the wife's dog after they had been kicking it around for ten years.

10

A man might use his approaching retirement as an excuse to write the children a letter, telling when he will retire, that he looks forward to it, that he and Mama are planning some wonderful times together. This will make the children a bit suspicious, of course, since they haven't had a letter from him since the sinking of the *Maine*. They won't even recognize his signature, since they haven't been getting any checks from him. What's the Old Man up to?

Still, he should write this letter, mailing it only after his wife has seen it. Then, about three weeks later, he should write the children a second letter. This will be the clincher. He should start the letter off with a report on what he plans to do with his leisure and with more details of what he and Mama are going to do together. Then he gets down to money, which is what the children have been holding their breath about since that first letter.

He should tell them he will get a nice pension and a good Social Security benefit (not saying how much). He should say that this income plus some savings he and Mama have managed will set them up very comfortably for retirement.

After this second letter, which if he isn't a heel he will also have shown his wife, he will get happy replies from all his children. The ice that has been forming these last twenty years will begin breaking up.

From this point on the father might get from his wife the names of the grandchildren. He heard them once, but he's forgotten. He might also find out how old each is.

Working always in unity with his wife, he might send a little gift to the family of each child, maybe in honor of his retirement. He might ask for new photographs of all the grandchildren for his billfold—he can't miss on this. He might inquire if his grandsons would like to do some fishing with Grandpa. Or go to a ball game.

After these preliminaries he can surely figure out how to move to win his children back. Or else he had better look for another Grandpa to play checkers with.

Cornering a Corner at Home

Be you man or woman, married or single, prepare in advance of retirement to set up a corner for yourself in the place where you live. It is to be your escape from the people around you, your private domain. It is to be your retirement office, and you'll need one.

This corner should have a desk ot sorts, which can be made out of a piece of plywood and four legs. On the desk should be what writing materials you use—typewriter, pen, pencils, paper, envelopes, paper clips, stamps. There should be a permanent chair, of course, because you don't want to drag one from the dining room every time you want to sit down. There should be some sort of enclosure, a file case, a drawer, or anything you can lock. In this enclosure go your bank book, your bills, your income tax and bank statements, your record of savings, handy data on your pension and Social Security, in fact anything in the way of business papers that does not go in the safety deposit box.

There are business affairs every retired person has to keep up with, which justifies your private corner from a practical standpoint. But there are going to be moments of boredom after you retire, and this corner nearly always can, or should, give you something to do. And there are going to be times when you long just to get away from the person or persons around you. The private corner provides this escape, and for this reason it should be out of sight of the living room, where most of the talking and most of the annoyances are. In a spare bedroom, the back hall, or the basement, perhaps.

Your Retirement Trip

You plan a trip, of course. Everybody does. And a big trip it will surely be, maybe to Yellowstone, because there's no job this time to hurry back to.

You are advised, even though it breaks your heart, that you shouldn't take this trip as soon as you retire. You should take it maybe five weeks later.

The simple magic of a new retirement—the not having to do anything, the wonder of looking at the outside world at 10 A.M. to 3 P.M., the breakfast at 9 A.M.—is elixir enough for the first few weeks. You can never quite recapture the magic of the first days of retirement if you have spent them buzzing down the highway. And, if you've gone away, you can never know what phone calls you got telling you what a mess things were in on the job since you left. Of course there would probably be no such calls, but the man or woman hasn't retired yet who didn't have delightful anticipation of some.

But there is a more serious reason for the delaying of the retirement trip. After about five weeks will come hangover of the new freedom, and with it the awful letdown as you realize that the job and all it meant to you are gone. The congratulations and good wishes are over. The old colleagues haven't found time yet to come by for a visit as they promised. The old job, with some very inferior individual now holding it, goes merrily on its way.

This is the hour, when the retirement impact hits hardest, that you should take off on your retirement trip. When you come back, you will have made some adjustments, and things will look better.

Saying Farewell to Your Job

Finally, with preparations made for the matters that have gone before, you come to the business of getting disengaged from your job, of stepping on the escalator that will take you out into the sunshine with a pension in your hand.

Manage this disengagement well and you will reap some practical benefits after you retire and will leave behind an "all right" image for years to come.

As a starter, if you have a job that carries a title, do all you can to pick your successor. It is the only sure way to be wonderful

13

after you're gone. Anybody who replaces you, as you must realize, will set out to do the job better than you did. This will often entail killing your ghost, which may mean pulling out of the files and showing to others the stupid decisions you made. A successor you have chosen will be human, too, and will have to prove he is better than you were. But he will remember for a while that you gave him the break and will not seek to smear your image.

Whether your job has been big or little, prepare to try a bit harder during your last weeks or months. You won't have to—bosses are aware that employees on the way out are inclined to let things slide. And in any case nobody on the way to retirement is ever fired. But you'll be regarded as a heel if you take advantage of the situation. You yourself will feel remorse later on.

Reassure all your old friends on the job that you will continue to see them after you retire, and that your friendship will go on as always. It won't, but your friends think it will and will like to hear you say it. Retirement is no arena for friends who still work, and job-connected friendships seldom wander over the pension line for long.

Pretend not to notice when your co-workers start planning a retirement party for you and go around asking donations for a retirement gift. Then when they surprise you with the announcement that they are giving you a retirement party, be surprised. Go to the party, saying all the while you don't deserve it, and when they present the retirement gift, accept it humbly, again saying you don't deserve it. When they ask you to get up and say something, get up and say the forecast for tomorrow is sunny and warm, then sit down. Nobody wants to hear you make a speech . . . not really. Don't get emotional. And if you feel impelled to get drunk, wait until you get home.

You come to the last day on the job. Don't try to be cute about it. The boss, if he's a good guy, will tell you to go before quitting time. Take him up on it. Say what good-byes you haven't said. Say them quietly and quickly. And be gone quickly. There's awkwardness to retirement good-byes.

Two

HANDLING YOUR FINANCES

Roger W. Matterson retired a few months ago with a pension of $195 a month, with Social Security for himself and his wife of $152 a month, and with paid-up life and health insurance from his company that was worth $15 a month.

With these three things Roger Matterson went into retirement richer than he had ever been in his life. He was, by any American standard, a wealthy man. He was worth $108,000.

It is quite possible that you are as rich as he was.

But to appreciate this fact you must develop a new perspective on money. As rich men have long known, a lot of money is a lot of paper—its value lies in what a lot of money will produce. A million dollars, for instance, is seldom that to a rich man. Instead, it is $40,000-a-year income, which he can get by investing the million at 4 percent.

The figure of 4 percent as used here is intended only as a basic return on invested money. The 4 percent, and occasionally 4½ percent, will be used throughout the book.

Interest and investment rates fluctuate, and no doubt will change many times over your lifetime. You can add or subtract a point or two on the basic 4 percent rate, according to what a safe investment pays at the time you invest.

All interest and investment rates in the book are on the low side, since the lower the return, as a rule, the safer the investment. And safety must be the prime consideration in a retirement nest egg that can't be replenished.

Any person at retirement time must realize that just as there are differences in investment returns, there are differences in types of investments—all the way from a bank savings account to a uranium mine. The uranium mine pays a higher return if it hits, just as money you invest in second mortgages pays you more than first mortgages, and third mortgages will pay you anything. All investments in this book are the conservative kind.

What a man gets in his retirement income is, in effect, the $40,000 gained from investing a million at 4 percent, or the income from a pile of money. In the Roger Matterson case, the total retirement benefit was $362 a month, or $4,344 a year. It would take just over $108,000, invested at 4 percent, to produce $4,344 a year. So Matterson had, in effect, the equivalent of $108,000 for the rest of his life.

Figure out just what your retirement income will be, then apply the 4 percent formula to it. You will be happy with what you find. If you will add your other resources to the figure you get— your $7,000 savings, the $4,000 cash value on your life insurance, and your $16,000 house—you will be happier still because you may discover that for all practical purposes you are an eighth of a millionaire.

Of course, since you can in no way get your hands on any part of your fortune but the four percent interest, problems in handling your retirement finances might crop up. It might, therefore, be wise to have a look at a couple of things.

The first is your retirement budget.

The best way to line that up is first to throw away all rules you ever heard on this subject, and then design a budget such as you never saw before. What you need in retirement is a budget that will bend to the way you want to live, not one that will make you bend to suit it.

For instance, you may be very sensitive about living at a fine address, but care very little for food. In this case, appropriate ten dollars for housing and ten cents for food. Or you may love steaks and be indifferent to the way you live. Then you reverse the figures.

People will tell you this is not the proper way to approach a budget. But most of them haven't yet been through the dramatic process of retirement.

In broad terms, a retired couple wanting to live the conventional lives of their working neighbors would appropriate about 25 percent of their income to housing and about 40 percent to food. But this doesn't make too much sense because the normal man starts eating less after he stops working, frequently giving up lunch. His children are grown and gone, and he and his wife have no need for the three bedrooms of twenty years ago, or even the dining room. Nor do they need to prove a point any longer—to maintain a nice home in a nice neighborhood.

Then there's the matter of clothing. In retirement there are days and days when white shirt and tie and the business suit gather dust in the closet.

Any way you figure it, the retired man or woman does not fit the conventional spending habits of other Americans and thus does not need a conventional budget.

An example of this is the budget for Mr. and Mrs. Walter B. Hunter. They enjoy a safe and pleasant retirement on an income of $325 a month:

HOUSING, *$125 a Month*

The Hunters wanted a city apartment. They figured, rightly, that in retirement they would sometimes be spending twenty-four hours a day in their home—more than anybody spends at home, except invalids—and that the home should therefore be more pleasant and more comfortable than working people require. Thus they decided to appropriate more than a third of their income, or $125 a month, to housing. The apartment is within walking distance of stores and a park, and is half a block from a bus line.

17

FOOD, *$50 a Month*

The Hunters, following retirement, went on a schedule of two meals a day. They have coffee and fruit juice when they arise in the morning, a breakfast-type meal at 10:00, and dinner at 5:30. They started making daily trips to the food market; they say they are eating well.

CLOTHING, *$15 a Month*

Money in this account has been accumulating since the Hunters retired. Mr. Hunter is still happy with the wardrobe he built up while he was working, seldom wears anything more formal than a pair of slacks, a sports shirt, and loafers with no socks. Mrs. Hunter has a sewing machine to remodel her clothes.

UTILITIES, *$15 a Month*

Heat and water are included in the apartment rent. The Hunters pay for electricity, gas, and phone.

HEALTH INSURANCE, *$15 a Month*

This is a private hospital plan to supplement Medicare.

TAXES, *$15 a Month*

No money has been taken from this account yet, but the Hunters figure that income taxes and personal property taxes will eventually take $15 a month.

PERSONAL ITEMS, *$10 a Month*

The Hunters went into retirement with a two-year supply of toothpaste, razor blades, toilet tissue, and soap, all bought out of salary before it stopped.

MEDICINES, *$10 a Month*

So far this money has been spent on dental work. They will let this account build up for the future.

AUTOMOBILE, *Nothing*

They decided they would be living close to most places, and could ride buses elsewhere. They also believed a couple on $325 a month couldn't afford a car with insurance and upkeep.

TRAVEL, *$25 a Month*

Twice a year the Hunters want to get out of town, usually to visit their children. This fund is to provide bus tickets or a rented car. They think that with their apartment-centered life, and without a car, a travel fund is necessary.

INCIDENTALS, *$20 a Month*

This covers cigars, beer, pocket change, and other small expenses that come up. The $20, in change, is placed in a fruit jar on a pantry shelf at the first of every month, and the Hunters draw on it as they need it.

19

EMERGENCIES, *$25 a Month*

This fund is to rescue any of the other funds that go over their limit, to meet any unexpected expenses, and to build a small household nest egg.

The Hunters keep books on their budget, and once each month balance all their accounts. The money set aside for clothing, taxes, travel, and emergencies—all sitting safely in the bank until needed—provides a cushion for all sorts of trouble that may come up. Or for a gay fling if the mood strikes them.

As a rule, retired people do not spend as much for housing as the Hunters do. They may still occupy the family home which, if it's worth $20,000, is costing them about $67 a month just to have that much money tied up (figuring that 4 percent rate again), in addition to taxes and upkeep. Or they may have grown accustomed to a certain standard of housing and don't want to give it up. But few go out deliberately and spend an outsize sum for housing on the grounds that they are going to be spending most of their hours at home from now on. Maybe they should. But the pressure for status, in housing, as in all else, eases off after retirement comes.

Relieved of the pressure of "having to make an appearance," many retired couples move into mobile homes that are parked in one of the many trailer parks located across the country. The mobile home may cost them $6,000. Others build or recondition living quarters in the side yards of their children. Some, moving to a warm climate, spend most of their time on the beach and in other outdoor activities. They are content with cheap housing that does no more than provide a place to eat, sleep, and watch television.

Food remains the constant expense. And food, no matter what they tell you, costs about the same everywhere. Citrus fruit comes cheaper in Arizona, corn in Iowa, ham in Georgia, coffee in Brazil. But these savings are inevitably offset by other commodities that must be brought in from far away.The only way to cut down on the food part of the budget is to (a) grow a garden and (b) roam the countryside and buy up meat and vegetables in large quantities from farmers, then store them in a freezer.

This saves money, but the city dweller is accustomed to government-inspected meats and washed vegetables in plastic wrappings. He has been buying these at the supermarket, and he is somewhat repelled by the native way of doing things. It's one of the penalties of being civilized.

The Hunters' ideas on the remainder of their budget are in line with the better thinking of most retired people, except for the automobile and the travel fund. They are probably right on the automobile; repairs, running expenses, insurance, and the cost of the constantly cheapening investment in a car are a serious drain on a modest retirement income. Most men have been kidding themselves too long on what a car costs. They have a difficult time convincing themselves, in retirement, that they can't afford the luxury anymore. Anyway, do you expect us to be heathens and walk?

Most retired people, by choosing housing that is close to public transportation, can eliminate a car and save enough money to rent one when they want it.

The travel fund of the Hunters is unique. But it is sensible since they don't have a car. And it is a good way to ensure that they will be able to visit their children at least once a year.

To sum up: A budget is not the same animal after retirement that it was before. Who cares now if your pants are shiny, or if the paint is peeling on your gutters, or how you live or where? So draw up a budget—you must have one—that provides for the new order of things. Make sure it provides that which will make you happiest.

And if anybody you know doesn't like it, tell him to write his Congressman.

Many people who are now retiring find the best way to handle a retirement budget is to move away from the town where the career has been, and get lost in sunshine country.

There are two logical reasons for their decision. One is that a couple is less embarrassed to cut its standard of living among strangers than among people "who knew them when." The other is that the normal couple has steadily increased its standard of living as income has risen over the years, and by age sixty-five has built-in expenses that can be shaken only by moving away.

The embarrassment factor is always more serious with couples who have engaged in an active social life. Clothes, entertainment, travel, expensive cars and homes, are key factors in such a life. Everybody notices if these trappings begin to fade away after retirement. And a couple's friends find it awkward, the same as the couple does. They grow reluctant to invite the couple to dinner parties that should be returned, or to invite them to affairs that will cost them money.

In time, most couples caught in this situation will quietly sell their home and move away, though originally they never intended to.

As for the built-in expenses, charitable contributions are the most notable example, though not usually the most expensive. When fund-raisers come to the door on their annual drives, they always want as much as the records show you gave last year, and usually ask for more. You find it difficult to offer less. The same with your church contributions.

Many couples, making good salaries during the working years, bought homes in keeping with their success. Maybe they were able to get them paid for before retirement. But the built-in costs of the home go on—air conditioning, yard service, paint jobs, insurance, and taxes. Sometimes the built-in necessity to own an automobile goes on because the better homes are frequently built beyond walking range of public transportation and stores.

Couples finding themselves saddled with built-in costs that cripple their pensions can always discard their "image," sell their home, and move to a lesser neighborhood. But this is far more difficult than to move into a lesser home and lesser neighborhood in a faraway town.

You might enjoy mulling for a couple of days over a quite

remarkable facet of your retirement income and budget. Both are the safest they have ever been in your life.

During your working years, you could be fired, merged, laid off, sent home by a strike, suspended, or laid low by a long illness. All of these would have cut or eliminated your income and jeopardized whatever budget you had.

In retirement, your income, and therefore your budget, are about as safe as mankind can make them. The Social Security is guaranteed by the United States Government, which will presumably be around if everything else fails; your pension and annuities are safeguarded by the most prudent investments in the land.

And while any income you made in your working years was subject to garnishments and other legal actions that could take it away from you, Social Security and pension checks are almost immune. Because, if for no other reason, courts are reluctant to let anybody tamper with the welfare of the retired.

You are probably going into retirement with a bit of money that is above and apart from your pension and your budget. A major step in the handling of your finances should be the exploitation of this money to bring you more income.

In general, and about in this order, here is where retired people are putting their savings:

        Savings and Loan Associations
        Savings Accounts in Banks
        U. S. Government Bonds
        Mutual Funds
        Common Stocks
        Preferred Stocks and Corporation Bonds

All of these are good and proper in certain circumstances. You will have to assess your circumstances from what follows.

Savings and Loan Associations

In recent years the savings and loan associations have come into great prominence in the country. They are now handling the savings of millions of people in all walks of life and of all ages, and are established in towns everywhere.

Your money, up to $20,000, is insured by the United States Government in a savings and loan account, provided the institution itself is insured. Most of them are. As a rule, you can withdraw your money from a savings and loan any time you want it if it is in a passbook account.

The return you can get on a savings and loan passbook account varies—from about 4 percent to about 5, depending on the area of the country where the institution is located. This return is paid twice a year, usually in June and December; or quarterly, usually starting in March; or annually, in December.

With retirement savings of $6,000, should you put them in a local savings and loan at 4 percent, or send them to one of the institutions located in another part of the United States which pay an average of about 5 percent?

A retired machinist, George Flannery, who had $6,000, went for the higher rate. He chose an institution from an advertisement in a New York financial journal, wrote a letter, and got back via airmail full particulars on an account, an account book, and a stamped, self-addressed envelope. He sent his money. Every three months thereafter he got a notice from the institution that so much return had just been declared, and that it had been added to his account.

"It was all right," Flannery said later, "and it was safe. But it wasn't much fun. I knew the people in the local savings and loan, could go up to argue with them, could get my money out if I needed it in a hurry. The save-by-mail thing was too impersonal. Anyway, the difference in return I was getting was $240 against $300 a year, or $5 a month. It wasn't enough to matter."

He moved his account back home.

Bank Savings Accounts

Bank rates on savings vary, but in most cases run about 4 percent on passbook accounts. Some retired people prefer banks because through the years they have come to trust them above most other institutions. Some, particularly women, have large sums in bank savings accounts and are well satisfied with the 4 percent return.

Here again your money is usually insured, and you can usually withdraw it any time you want it. You usually collect interest once or twice a year.

Savings of $6,000 in a bank at 4 percent, as compared with a savings and loan at 5 percent, would be a difference of $5 a month.

Both banks and savings and loans began offering on a wide scale in the 1960's what they called Certificates of Deposit, or Saving Certificates, or some such. They pegged the return on these certificates slightly higher than on passbook accounts and in return specified that the money be left on deposit for a particular period of time, usually ninety days or six months.

U. S. Government Bonds

The return on government bonds will vary somewhere between the passbook return of a bank and a savings and loan. (This is on the popular type of bonds. Some issues pay more.) The mechanics of buying and cashing bonds are somewhat cumbersome, and the figuring of interest is involved. But many people now reaching retirement have been buying government bonds off and on during their working years. They feel comfortable with them. They know they can cash them at any time, and they know they are safe.

Mutual Funds

Savings and loans, banks, and government bonds are for those who can't stand to lose their retirement savings. The savings remain static through inflation and deflation, which can be bad or good. Mutual funds, on the other hand, are for those who can

25

afford to lose some of what they've got. The more popular funds are not static, but go up or down depending on the fund's skills and on the fortunes of American business.

There are many kinds of mutual funds—"growth funds," "income funds," "conservative funds," and others. The one the retired person would buy would probably be an income fund, composed of stocks and bonds of American corporations. The shares you hold in a fund can usually be cashed in at any time, at whatever the market value of the shares is at the moment. Dividends are usually paid quarterly.

Mutual funds, as you probably know, are a wide collection of stocks and/or bonds that have been placed in one big basket. You buy a part of the basket. Thus if part of the securities go bad, the others are supposed to cushion the loss so you won't be hurt too much.

You don't get mutual funds for free. On most of them you pay a commission when you buy your shares, and this runs up to 7 percent or better, which means that on $6,000 you would pay about $420 for the privilege of buying. But for this commission you are buying professional investment experts to handle the money. They are supposed to be good. If they are, your $6,000 can grow to $10,000. Your return can be 6 percent or better. If business goes to pot, you can lose your shirt.

For people who can afford a reasonable gamble with their savings, and who want to share in the growth of business, mutual funds are probably their best bet.

But go to a reputable broker and buy your mutual funds. Don't let somebody come to your door and sell them to you.

Common Stocks

The normal retired person has about as much business investing his savings in individual common stocks as he has sticking his finger in a fire. If he can spend about five hours a day studying the stock market, has some savvy about corporations, keeps informed on business and management changes, he may do all right. Otherwise he would do better fishing.

Preferred Stocks and Bonds

Investments in preferred stocks and bonds are for the rich. And if you are rich, you are already playing golf with wealthy brokers who have already sold you some. You know your way through the intricacies of such investments.

There are other things retired people can do with their money: hide it in a mattress, behind a mirror, under a floorboard, in a partition, and in a tin can in a hole behind the garage. More people than you know do this.

Money placed in tin cans, in savings and loans, banks and bonds usually loses nothing in face value. It also usually gains nothing, which is not so nice if serious inflation comes. The mutual funds composed mainly of common stocks, and individual common stocks, can lose value. They can also gain it.

You often hear some pretty stories of people getting 6 and 7 percent on their investments. It happens, but seldom on the kind of safe investments a retired person should have.

Your Life Insurance

Life insurance calls for some of your better financial management in retirement. If you are a man and are like most men, you bought your life insurance between ages twenty-five and forty-five. You bought it for the specific purpose of protecting your young wife and babies in case you died. This was a good and noble cause. The trouble is, you didn't die.

You bought policies that required premium payments for twenty years, or until age sixty-five, or maybe for life. So through all these years you have been paying. Now, with retirement on you, you possess just what you asked for thirty years ago—protection of a young wife and children. But your wife is flirting with Social Security, and the babies are grown and gone.

And you're still hanging around.

So take out your policies and just for the novelty read them. You won't understand them; nobody but a lawyer can. But in all the fine print and the whereas clauses you will get the idea that maybe now you can do something with the policies besides dying for them.

You can, for instance, convert them into an investment that is more meaningful to a retired man. At least you can on most policies. In the world of finance, life insurance people are among the good guys. They won't cheat you, and they'll be helpful. They want to hold on to your money. But they will tell you any special advantages your policies have for you now.

The first possible advantage is that you may be able to stop paying premiums at sixty-five, even though you have life-pay policies. A second advantage is that you may be able to convert the policies into a paid-up annuity that will provide you a monthly payment at age sixty-five or sixty-eight. A third advantage is that you can turn the policies in for a nice bundle of cash.

The annuity route is a good one for most retired people. The annuity can provide monthly income for life, the size of the payment depending on your age and the value of your policies. It can provide a monthly income for life for your wife, starting when you retire, when you die, or whenever you want.

There are many kinds of annuities, and only your insurance company can explain them to you properly. Your wife's brother can't. Neither can the fellow at the filling station.

There is the little matter of your dying that you might consider. Your insurance policies would be expected to provide the cash for that. So, whatever you do in converting your policies, you might see that money is set aside for this. Social Security contributes a couple of dollars to this cause, but it hardly covers the tips on what some widows pay to lay their husbands away. If you are not too vain about the matter, you can maneuver some important money into your widow's hands by writing out now just what kind of expensive funeral you don't want, and leaving the document where it can be found. This won't buy the undertaker many Cadillacs, but it will buy your widow some groceries.

There are some occasions when it is wise for a man to cash in his life insurance at sixty-five, but only if his wife has other provisions for support in case he dies.

For example, you can come up to retirement with a mortgage still on your house. You can manage to continue the monthly payments out of your pension, but just barely. The mortgage is going to take the fun out of your life for the next six years. But your wife, if you leave her behind, will have Social Security and a part of your pension you have set aside for her. These come to $150 or so a month. With the house she can do nicely with that—without the mortgage. So cash the insurance, pay off the mortgage, and give yourselves six pleasant years together, instead of leaving her an embarrassing hunk of insurance money she won't know what to do with anyway.

A trip to Europe, a cabin on a lake, winter trips to the sunshine—all sorts of dreams can be realized from the money you have built up in life insurance policies that no longer have a valid role in your life. Just so you won't need it as a retirement nest egg, and your widow won't need it when you're gone.

Beware of Mortgages

The largest piece of money retired people ever see is the check they get for their home, when and if they sell it and move away. It was by far the largest piece a fellow named Ritchie ever saw. He wasn't about to let it get out of his hand, either.

The Ritchies were moving to Florida and would buy another home there. They wound up with a net of $16,500 from the sale of their old home, and Ritchie promptly went down to the local savings and loan and deposited $14,000 of it at 4½ percent. He was holding out $2,500 as a down payment on the new home in Florida.

The Ritchies bought a home for $14,000 in Florida. In the price, of course, was a 6 percent commission to the man who sold them the house, making it a $13,160 house. Because of a down payment of only $2,500, and because of his age, Mr. Ritchie didn't get a very good mortgage. After all the fees and fiddle-faddle were figured in he was paying around 9 percent interest.

But his pension could handle the monthly payments (for ten years), and he had that $14,000 in the S. & L., by golly!

There are ways to manage your money in retirement. This is not one of them.

In the first place, the Ritchies were getting 4½ percent for their own money, and paying 9 percent to borrow somebody else's. This is not a good way to get rich. The loss was in the neighborhood of $50 a month.

Finally, why? The money in the savings and loan wasn't doing anything for them; they could always borrow later on their paid-for house if an emergency arose. And the fuss and bother of taking out a mortgage and writing 120 monthly checks over the next ten years are not chores a retired man should take on.

There is a notion in the land that it is wise to have a mortgage on your house because it makes it easier to resell the house. This may be true. But in twenty-five years of looking, the author has never seen such a case.

It is all right to sell your house and buy a new one after you retire. In fact, if it's what you want, you ought to do it. Just don't delude yourself—it is one of the most costly operations you ever undertake. The fees and commissions you pay twice, in selling and buying, are large. The cost of moving furnishings is high. The losses from what you discard because you don't want to move too much—and the prices you pay in the new location for things you must replace, including new draperies and rugs—are invariably large.

Few retired people would ever sell, move, and buy if first they figured out exactly what the cost is.

Now don't let all this discourage you, because you might come out of such an operation as a sharp fellow on Long Island did when he retired to Louisiana. When he sold his house, he netted $15,000. He wanted to rent quarters in Louisiana for a year before buying a new home but didn't want his $15,000 to lie idle, so he invested it in the common stock of one of the top United States corporations. The stock was selling for $56 a share.

When he was ready to buy the new house, his stock was going steadily up in price, and he didn't want to sell it. He went to a bank, put the stock up as collateral, borrowed $11,000, and went out and bought his new house for cash.

A few months ago the price of his stock had gone to $102 a share. He sold it and pocketed nearly $12,000 profit. He had to pay a sizable tax on the profit. Even so, he virtually got his new house for free. He paid off the bank and went happily on his way.

That stock he bought, you understand, could also have gone down $46 a share.

Saying No to the Children

The time comes now for a look at the most emotionally charged facet of managing your money in retirement. It is the toughest: How to pass your money to your children.

One premise in this matter, no matter how many variations in circumstances there are, is unassailable and eternal. This premise is that:

> Older parents who have money to give are beautiful and wonderful and magic creatures;
> Older parents who have already given it are older parents.

From this premise you may draw the conclusion that the longer you restrain yourself, the longer you put off giving away what you have, the longer you will be wonderful.

Some parents have been wonderful for their entire lifetimes through the rather bizarre technique of giving away virtually none of their money until they were in the cemetery and a lawyer read their wills.

Children of retired people are, first, people; and second, children. And they love money. By the time parents retire, children are usually in their forties. This is the age not just to love money but to adore it. What with children going to college, Daddy bucking for a vice-presidency, and such.

31

What are retired parents to do when their children need some of their savings, or when they come with some brashness to ask for a loan? Solomon couldn't supply the answers, because parents, it seems, love their children. Their lives usually center on the children after retirement. And, anyway, the children are going to get the money in the end, aren't they?

No rules can govern all situations, but retired parents who have stuck firmly to the policies set out below have always fared best:

1. Never tell your children how much money you have.
2. Never tell your children for sure that you will leave them your money.
3. Do not let yourself believe your children are entitled to your money. They aren't.
4. Give some money to your children in your lifetime if you can afford to, but never a major part of it and never on any regular basis lest they begin to expect it.
5. Beware of jealousy among your children if you have more than one. Children (or their spouses) can grow violent when they think any one child is getting more from you than they are.
6. Be extremely cautious about granting a loan to a child. If the child is a good credit risk, he or she can borrow money from a bank. If not a good risk, why should you —and the other heirs—be patsies?
7. Draw up wills for both the husband and the wife, leaving what you have equally to all children. No matter if one has been better or worse than the others, if you hope to keep the children together as a family, you can't be partial with money. Kisses, maybe. Money, no.

THREE

~~~~~~~~

CHOOSING A PLACE TO LIVE

You are one of the adventurous souls who plan to pull up stakes, chip your initials out of the sidewalk, and move away when you retire. Maybe to Florida.

That's a pleasant dream to fondle. So fondle it. But about two months before the pension and the moving van come, sit down and write yourself a letter, along the following lines:

Dear Me:

This letter is intended to be read about four months after you move into the new town, or at the point of deepest depression after you move in—whichever comes first.

Four months will be about it. The Welcome Wagon will have come and gone. The parson will have made his duty call. The neighbors will have brought their cookies. The natives who thought you might be interesting will have sized you up. The merchants and service people will have made their pitch.

And where have all these people gone?

Gloom will have invaded your retirement home, through the windows where no neighbor yells for a cup of sugar; through the doors where nobody rings the bell; even through the telephone, which doesn't ring.

This letter, written well in advance, is to insist to you

33

that this situation is normal and that it comes to almost every retired couple moving to a new town.

This is not a time to panic, to curse the day you decided you wanted to move, to damn this cold and friendless town, or to think of moving again. You made your decision to come here with a sound mind. It was probably a good decision. Stick with it. Because the situation will pass in three months or so if you move aggressively into community life now—and start joining things. In about a year if you wait for nature to take its course. It's just the way towns are— organized and self-sufficient before you ever show up and really in no dire need of you until you have time to make yourself needed.

In brief, this letter seeks to tell you what the doctor tells the expectant mother: "There is going to come a time when it hurts . . . just bear with it for a little while and everything will be all right."

[signed] *Myself*

This is one reason why those of little faith should take a closer look at their dream of moving away. But there are others, more important, that even those with courage should ponder. Here they are:

ONE.   Children and grandchildren are usually the most precious possessions of a retired couple. The old family home, if the children grew up there, is a shrine of sorts to them. Most of them retain for life an image of the home as a place of goodness and joy, and of wonderful memories. It lures them back for visits. Would a concrete-block house in the sun, even with a tangerine tree in the backyard, substitute for this image?

TWO.   Children, with little ones, are usually running a dollar short, because expenses run high now for a growing family. These children are inclined to welcome a summer vacation back home, where the kiddies can sleep in the room that was Daddy's, but more pertinent, where the rooms are free, the kitchen is available, and maybe the freezer is stocked. Would the concrete house have

34

extra rooms for the clan? If not, how far is the nearest motel and what would it cost per night, with three meals a day, for a child, a spouse, and three kiddies? When they don't have any money to spare in the first place?

THREE.   Granting that the children of a retired couple think the old homeplace is a dump anyway, and granting that they have enough money to come visiting and stay in a motel, will it be practical for them to get from where they are to where you are going? Many children nowadays flock to the larger cities of the North and the East and to California.

Retired people who move usually flock to the southern rim of the United States. A child working, say, in Chicago, might fly his family to Miami or Los Angeles. But if the child is working one hundred miles out of Chicago, and the retired parents are living one hundred miles from Miami, the time and the nuisance of making a visit would in time make the whole thing seem just too much. The practice of retired parents has been to move to small towns that are off the main airline routes, off the superhighways, and to the faraway. Few factors have been more significant in weakening, if not breaking, close ties between retired parents and their children.

FOUR.   It is very costly to move from one town to another. And you should not make the mistake—which most retired people make—of believing that the cost of the moving van is about it.

There is the cost of replacing in the new town the old things in the home you chose not to move. Most importantly, there is the large and continuing cost of services you can no longer get at a bargain rate. If the air-conditioning system broke down back home, you knew a fellow who would fix it with a wire and a couple of washers for $2.50. In the new town you'll need a new condenser. In the old town, a friend at the service station would fix the car carburetor with a screwdriver for free; in the new town it's a garage job, for $14. In the old town, the doctor and dentist had had you around for a long time, knew your condition and circumstances, and billed you accordingly. In the new town, good luck!

Don't get discouraged now. If your heart is set on moving when you retire, there are some splendid reasons for doing it, and these will be cited shortly. The purpose of what you are reading is to lay out the good and the bad of all the moves you make in retirement, without trying to sell you any of them—which is a sort of treatment retired people seldom get. You should learn the negative factors of what you plan, and the positive factors. You should then apply them all to your particular circumstances and make up your mind. You may make a wrong decision, but if you understand what is being written here you at least are not going to be surprised when some of the retirement facts of life come up to slap you in the face.

FIVE.   If you move to a new town as a man and wife, you will be setting up a life for a couple. Which is natural. But what is the wife or the husband going to do if one or the other dies in this faraway place in a year and a half? This is a vital question. Few retired people will answer it. Before you move, answer it.

SIX.   In moving to a new town at age sixty-five or so, you do not have the personal magnetism to attract friends to your hearth. Nor do you have the status that attracts them. The curve of a hip or the cut of a moustache doesn't matter now. And gray-haired charm doesn't compete too well with television or a nap. As for status, the influence to do things for others and the contacts that would help others promote themselves have passed. You should face up to these things, even if you don't like to read them, and thereupon should base your prospects of making friends in your new town. You can make friends in the new town, some good and lasting ones, but you must *make* them, which means you must work at it for maybe a year or two, and meanwhile expect no visitors at the hospital if you have an operation.

On the Other Hand . . .

The dream of traveling, or moving away to a prettier town, is probably the strongest dream of those approaching retirement— stronger than the yen to escape from work or to sit in leisure. It is a dream that needs some sort of fulfillment, lest the person retiring feel forever after that life has cheated a little.

This dream is one of the strongest arguments for moving away when the pension comes. And it will allow you—as some arguments won't—to make a trial run of the adventure.

Suppose, for instance, that Arizona has bugged you over the recent years. You long to move there and ride tall across the desert, and as any fool would know it will be w-o-n-d-e-r-f-u-l for your health. You have $4,500 in savings, your $15,000 house is paid for, and your pension and Social Security will bring you a comfortable $325 a month. You can afford to move. You want to. So you're going to sell out, pick up, and take off.

Well, that's not the way to do it.

You probably don't know much about Arizona if you haven't lived there. You have built your dream on a book you read, on the movies, on somebody's sales pitch, and maybe on a couple of two-week vacations there. You can't know what Arizona is like—about the preciousness of water and the oppression of heat. You can't afford to gamble the rest of your life—because you don't *have* to go; you are riding a dream—on a location that may make you miserable.

So, get in touch with the officials of any grade school or college in reasonable distance of your home. Say you would like to lease your home, furnished, to several teachers or to a teacher's family for the nine months of the school term. You can get such tenants if your rental is sensible. Of course you may have to wait until the next September comes around. But what's your hurry—you've got no bus to catch.

The money you get from the lease, plus your $325, will set you up quite comfortably in Arizona for a year. Not because prices will be any cheaper—they won't be—but because there are many opportunities there to lower your standard of living without pains. Many people who came from backgrounds as good as yours are living contentedly there on incomes as low as $300 a month.

If you find that the cost of traveling to and from Arizona and the standard of living you want to try will strain the income you have, you would be wise to take up to $1,000 from your savings to finance the experiment. If the move could prove to you, for sure, that Arizona is—or is not—the place for you, the $1,000 would be a bargain price.

When a year is up, return to the old hometown, look at it through the wiser eyes you now have, and make up your mind. It is best that you not make the decision in either the disgust or the joy of Arizona, whichever it may be, but back in the old hometown from which your strength came. If the decision is to move, then sell the house, conduct yourself as if you are saying good-bye for good because you probably are, pack up, and go. If the decision is to stay, then reclaim your home and be forever thankful for the mistake you didn't make.

There are practical reasons why a retired person or couple should shake off the dust of the old town and get along to a new one as soon as the pension comes. They follow here, with some suggestions on how each situation may best be handled.

ONE. You are embarrassed because you no longer have a job. Men, especially, can fall into this situation, and they can forfeit most of their due pleasures of retirement unless they get away from it. Men as a rule have all their prestige tied into their jobs. They hold a union office, belong to a business organization, go to luncheon clubs, head this committee or that, sit at speakers' tables, and travel to conventions—all because of the job they hold. Retirement cuts most of these ties, sometimes slowly and sometimes at once. And men, who are invariably vainer than women, find it a difficult ordeal—more difficult, in fact, than the breaking of the ties at the company. It was the extracurricular activities that put the whipped cream on the pie.

Then there is the loss of friends, most of whom for both men and women are co-workers at the company. The friendships don't die because there is often deep fraternity among those who have worked side by side through the years. But they have to tread water because those who are still at the lathe simply don't have time to be playmates to those who are retired.

When a man and woman feel embarrassment because there are no more trappings, or because the old friends don't come around too often, it is usually best that they move on to a new hunting ground.

Once there, relinquish the hold of the old life while setting out to make the new one.

There is no cause for bitterness if you should find yourself after retirement in the situations cited here. Many other people have gone through them, and have come to understand that, as people, they are no less capable, no less loved, than they were before. The whole thing is a natural by-product of retirement.

Two. You are uncomfortable because of your income. Retirement always brings a sharp drop in spendable income. Not so much as most people think, but enough to cause some changes in your way of life. You have figured in advance that you can adjust well enough to these changes, but once you are four months out into retirement you discover that the adjusting becomes awkward with neighbors looking on through their curtains.

Of course it's not quite that crude. But you get the point. Neighbors who have known you for a long time know your habits and your likes or dislikes. It is obvious to them when you start changing your ways, and it is obvious why: The pension is pinching. When, added to this, they see your gutters going longer without paint, your less-affluent grocery cart at the market, your shoes being half-soled instead of discarded, the neighbors in their goodness seek to help—by not asking you to play golf, not giving you invitations you'll have to repay, not suggesting any sort of joint affairs that might cost you money.

Not all retired people feel this awkwardness about money among their neighbors. But many do. And when they do they can solve it best by moving to a new community. To a town that cannot compare.

Some men who have had active friends in business find when they retire that they don't, that there is a gradual decline in the relationships. The sports affairs, fishing trips, drinking parties, etc., can't easily bridge the gap between a salary and a pension.

As a rule, a retired person or couple moving into a new town is taken at face value. If they drive into town in a Cadillac, they are rich; if they arrive in a 1960 Ford, they aren't, very. Housing, clothes, and entertaining as well as the car readily stamp new-comers in a town as affluent, modest, or pushed. The natives aren't too interested in probing the matter beyond that, or finding out how rich the newcomers were back home. They'll take what they see, and can make no comparisons with the past.

So, in moving to the new town it is usually wise to set yourself up a couple of notches below the status you can afford. Then over the next two years move up to where you belong.

THREE. You can't shake your built-in expenses in the old town. Over the years, people are inclined to get themselves steadily involved in larger overhead expenses. This is natural; the income has been going up steadily. At retirement time, as a rule, it is the highest of your working career. And all around you are expenses you have taken on because of that income.

Most serious of these expenses is usually the house you live in and the standard of life you have set up in it. A $30,000 house might be in line for a couple with a salary income. It is the base of operations for the job. It's a reasonably sized investment for a good salary. It's probably manageable on upkeep costs.

But most retirement incomes can't afford the upkeep on a $30,000 house, which of course is the oldest now it has ever been. Most retired people, with small savings, have no business with $30,000 invested in any one thing. And in retirement the house is no longer the powerhouse behind the job and the salary.

Apart from the upkeep, the taxes, insurance, and all the rest that go with a $30,000 house, there is the unhappy truth that it costs you about $110 a month for it just to sit there. This is what you could get per month if you sold the house and invested the $30,000 at 4½ percent.

You will find it difficult to get out from under the expenses of your house if you stay in town. A lesser house would be an embarrassment to you. It might well embarrass your friends. It very probably would mean moving to a lesser part of town.

Wives of retired men sometimes face some difficult problems on the house matter. They have expanded their social activities as the husband has grown in importance on the job, as the children have grown up and left them more leisure. Frequently they belong to clubs, have parties at home, have visitors in. The house is part of their image. They cannot easily agree to swap it for a lesser image, on another street.

But they can often agree to break the whole thing off, and move into a house they can properly afford, if it is in a new town among people who didn't know them before.

There are other built-in expenses. There are club dues, and if the club is golf or social, the dues are just the beginning of the costs. To pull out of clubs because of retirement would not look good. To pull out because you are moving to a new town would. There is your contribution to the church. It needs as much as you gave last year, and a little more if you can. All the charity drives—Community Fund, Cancer, Red Cross, TB, Heart Fund, Playground Association, and all the rest—also have records on you and need a little more this year.

The normal retired person just doesn't want to stand at the front door and tell some neighbor or friend he or she can't afford to give as usual. But such a person can move out of town, where they don't have records and comparisons, and wipe the slate clean on these obligations.

FOUR.   The neighborhood where you live is showing wear. People usually come up to retirement in a neighborhood where they have lived a long time, or in a house they bought twenty years ago and have finally paid for. From about age fifty-five on they don't switch housing much.

But the neighborhood is not the same one it was when you chose it several years ago, particularly if it is in a city. There have been changes, and they have usually been for the worse, though there are exceptions. The character of neighbors usually changes as a neighborhood declines. Young families with the ambition and energy to improve things veer away to a fresh suburban street.

So, if the time has come at retirement when it would be desirable for you to move to a better community anyway, why not ride the dream to sunshine country?

FIVE.   You have grown weary of the problems at home. The taxes won't quit. There are labor troubles. Social problems are

41

everywhere. There's too much snow to shovel. The windstorms and the rain keep returning. The politicians are no good. The streets are too crowded. The mosquitoes are bad.

By retirement age many people have had enough of their tired old problems. They long to escape them, and frequently figure that to move from this town to another one, though there will be problems still, the new ones will be a refreshing swap.

Where to Move, If You Move

The most popular areas for retirement, about in this order, are:
FLORIDA, from Orlando south
CALIFORNIA, mostly in the southern part
ARIZONA, around Phoenix and Tucson
NORTH CAROLINA, mostly in the mountains around Asheville
THE GULF COAST, including Mississippi, Louisiana, and Texas
ARKANSAS, all over
THE RIO GRANDE VALLEY, at the Southeastern border of Texas
MEXICO, along the west coast
Nobody can tell you whether any of these is a good retirement area. It depends entirely on how you like it and how your personality meshes into the landscape. There are a few general guidelines, however, to each area. They will give you an indication of what you'll find. Choose the guidelines you like and you can go to the public library and get a three hundred-page book or two that will tell you everything about the area from its pollen count to its water level.

FLORIDA has to be a pretty good retirement area. All those Yankees can't be wrong. It has a climate older people seem to like, though it gets as hot as blazes at times. There is seldom a freeze south of Orlando. There are bugs, including mosquitoes. There is mildew. There are hurricanes. Whatever its faults, Florida has developed over the years an atmosphere retired people like.

In almost every town it caters to retired people.

For retirement purposes, there are two Floridas: the west

coast and the central lake region where the middle-class American has been inclined to settle, both in the cities such as St. Petersburg and Tampa and in the small towns; and the east coast from Palm Beach to Miami where the richer Americans go. But there's a mixture, and you can find the $300 pension and the $20,000-a-year stock dividends in all areas.

CALIFORNIA is more glamorous than Florida for retirement, and it, too, has to be pretty good because all those Midwesterners can't be wrong. While Florida in general is placid, California tends to bustle. And Southern California, where many retirees go, bustles fast and noisily. The climate is moderate, and nearly everybody likes it. There's rain. There's fog. There have been earthquakes and brush fires. California has more jobs than Florida, because there is more industry. It has more young people, more fluid politics. Retirement living runs the gamut from trailers to mansions, as it does in Florida. Costs are about the same as in Florida. California is a long way from everything except the Pacific Ocean. You would not feel at home as quickly there as in Florida.

ARIZONA is a hot, dry country with wind. Deserts are all around. Phoenix and Tucson are the major cities, and most retired people have settled in or around them. There are many trailer parks. Standards of living might be somewhat lower here than in Florida or California. Arizona is reputed to have many health-giving virtues, particularly its sunshine. To the average Midwesterner or Easterner, the general atmosphere of Arizona would be more difficult to adjust to than that of most other areas. The scarcity of water is a constant problem, and it influences what you have in your garden, your yard, and your scenery.

NORTH CAROLINA has usually been regarded around the country as a place for the rich to retire to. For years Asheville and Southern Pines have attracted the rich, and both cities have retirement mansions and exclusive resorts. Things are breaking down now, and in the smaller towns along the edge of the Alleghenies in western North Carolina the $300 and $400 pension set is moving in in large numbers. The state has a moderate climate, a change of seasons that includes cold winters and hot summers. It is trying to attract northern industries, has good roads and lots of pine trees.

THE GULF COAST has never promoted itself as a retirement paradise to the extent other areas have. There are few towns anywhere along the coast that are well known as retirement towns, yet in most of them are couples who have moved in with pensions from somewhere else. The climate is pleasant, the sun hot. There is much fishing. In some of the smaller towns a pension will travel far because there is not too much to buy, and the economic levels are low. The area extends from Mobile, Alabama through Mississippi, Louisiana, and Texas, all the way down to Brownsville.

ARKANSAS as a retirement country is, in the main, rural. People in rather large numbers have gone there to buy a piece of land and raise chickens (not too profitably), or to acquire a rustic hideaway. Men in the cities who can still smell the new-mown hay from their boyhood on a farm are drawn to Arkansas when they retire. Climate is moderate. Standards of living outside the cities are low. Arkansas is one of the southern states that are yanking at their economic bootstraps.

THE RIO GRANDE VALLEY has a river, the Rio Grande, except when it dries up. It has many people of Mexican descent, a hot climate, some pleasant towns, and a lot of retired farm owners from Iowa and Nebraska. Housing is modest, and includes trailers. A $200 pension will get you by there well enough. And you'll have plenty of good vegetables to eat, along with pink grapefruit and oranges. The Valley is a long way from everywhere, except Mexico.

MEXICO continues to be a major lure to retiring Americans. Largely, one suspects, because somebody once said you can have a lot of servants there for about ten dollars a week. Which you can. But not much else. Americans retired to Mexico live mainly along the western coast, maintain standards of living on a par with California, and one way or another pay about as much for it as they would in California. Cheap living in Mexico comes when you live as the Mexicans do. Most Americans won't. Mexico, being a foreign country, can be lonely for a retired American who does not belong to one of the usually exclusive American colonies that are set up in the better coastal cities.

You can move to any of these areas, with the exception of Mexico, and find retired people there from your home state. Frequently you will find state societies organized, with the Pennsylvania Pensioners and the Connecticut Codgers, or some such, competing in shuffleboard and bridge. In some of the areas, particularly Southern California and Florida, you will find that retired employees of certain large corporations have banded together in their own communities.

So, if you seek to find in these areas a retirement town that hasn't already been explored by somebody from your home area, you will be disappointed. If you seek to be among people with your own language and your own regional views, which is more likely, you can't miss.

In the main, people who have retired to the areas cited above have been seeking a more satisfying climate and a lower cost of living. Are these what you want? Might there be other factors that would bring the golden years more firmly into your parlor? Here are factors to consider:

Climate

Climate isn't what it's cracked up to be. It never has been. Warm climate is warm, and nice. But if it is warm, it will usually get hot, and in some of the popular retirement areas you can expect for part of the year to flee indoors about 11 A.M. and stay there out of the sun until about 4 P.M. This is all right— it won't kill you—but it is important that you know this facet of sunshine country which hasn't been advertised much.

Those who have moved into Florida, Arizona, and Texas have enjoyed their warm hours, and learned to adjust to the hot ones. You can, too. Just don't go to the places expecting to find a climate that is much more satisfying to you than what you are leaving behind.

45

After a while, as a matter of fact, you aren't going to pay much attention to the climate, any more than you will to the scenery.

Cost of Living

The cost of living is just about the same everywhere in the United States and Mexico as it is in your hometown *if you maintain the same standard of living you now have.*

You should be repeatedly warned of this, because the illusion that somewhere else will cost less money than here has trapped more retired people into a financial crisis than anything else.

You can live more cheaply on an Arkansas farm than you can in a Pittsburgh suburb. But you may not have a sealed house, a sewage system, a hospital, or access to the food and medicines and merchandise the stores in Pittsburgh offer you.

You can live more cheaply in a trailer in an Arizona park than you can in a five-room brick apartment in New Jersey. It's not the same standard of living. Neither is a bungalow on a Class C street in St. Petersburg the same standard as a split-level on a Class A street in Cincinnati.

You get what you pay for. All the time. Everywhere. And if you let anybody sell you sunshine country because of the low price of citrus fruit and the elimination of a furnace—without asking what steaks cost and how much an air-conditioning unit is— you are heading into a trap.

Of course, as stated earlier, many retired people can bring themselves to lower their standard of living when they move away from the old town, but couldn't if they stayed on. That's all right, so long as they know they are doing this instead of thinking they are getting a bargain.

If the climate and cost of living are less than perfect as reasons for choosing a retirement town, how then can you go about making this critical decision?

You can follow the blueprint laid out by a retired couple, Mr. and Mrs. Edward R. Wren, who moved from New York State to a town near Galveston on the Texas Gulf Coast.

They liked Texas. They liked the water facilities around Galveston. So, with this area in mind they first got what data they could from an encyclopedia. They then wrote the chambers of commerce in Galveston and other surrounding towns asking for any free literature on the towns. They wrote the Office of the Governor in Austin, the capital, asking that any departments of the state send any material available on the Galveston region. (Information from chambers of commerce and state government offices is usually reliable, but none of it is about to tell you anything wrong about their area. It also seldom gets down to the nuts and bolts of retirement living that you want.)

According to Mr. Wren, "We digested the encyclopedia data and the literature from Texas, then went to the public library and listed all books that would throw any light on our prospective new home. One by one we took these books out of the library, and Mrs. Wren and I took turns reading them aloud to each other."

He realized, he said, that the information they were compiling, while good, was not sufficient for a decision on moving so far away. In the end they would have to visit Galveston.

"We had started our research about a year before my retirement date," Mr. Wren explained, "so we decided we would take my last three-week vacation for the visit. Driving would be cheaper, but would take too much time from our visit and be too tiring.

"We weren't able to spend this sort of money, what with a pension coming on. But the more we thought about it, the more we figured we couldn't afford not to. This was one of the most important steps we had ever made, going so far to establish a new home which in all probability would be home for the rest of our lives. Even if we didn't like it we probably would be stuck with it for life. It would be out of the question ever to finance a move back to New York, and it is doubtful there would ever again be much there for us, once we had packed up and moved."

They arranged to squeeze the salary for part of the cost, and take the rest out of savings.

They flew to Houston, rented a car at the airport, and started a grand tour of the towns to the south and toward Galveston. There were ten days of this, at about thirty dollars a day (excluding the car). They then returned the car to Houston, took a bus to the town that had looked most promising to them, registered at a downtown motel, and began looking.

"In anything but the larger cities, there are two specific hours during which you should take a hard look at a town you are about to choose. One is between 10 and 11 A.M. on a weekday, when the town is alive. The other is between 8 and 9 P.M. on a Monday night, when it is dead. These are the extremes, and you can figure the life you'll find here will be somewhere between the two."

These are the primary things the Wrens checked:

- Display windows of the better women's dress shops, to determine whether it was a hick town or a smart town. Few things will tell you quicker.
- Three supermarkets, to determine which foods were cheaper and which were more expensive, in order to compare with the overall costs back home.
- Interest paid on savings by the local banks and savings and loan associations, to see if they should switch their accounts when they moved.
- The fees charged by doctors for an office call, the availability of hospitals and nursing homes.
- The reliability of local bus transportation from residential areas to the shopping district, in case they later wanted to give up their car.
- The taxes they would have to pay, not just now but all the way to the cemetery, including sales, state income. intangibles, gasoline, and state inheritance. (Taxes, like food, pretty well balance out from one region to another, and again you get what you pay for. You don't really have to have fire stations and paved streets.)
- The matter of tourists and vacationists, since the Wrens had come to believe that any town catering hard to the traveling trade would be inclined to make local residents and pensioners eat at the second table.

- The direction the town was moving, in order to choose their home in a section where the better people were settling. ("It's funny," Mr. Wren said, "but nearly every town in the country develops northward, which means you don't want to get stuck with housing on the southern side.")
- The economic well-being of the people living in the better section of town, in order to determine how their retirement income might stack up with that of their future neighbors. This they did by walking down the residential streets, appraising the costs of the houses, as compared to costs back home; seeing how many bathrooms they had by observing the vents on the roofs; how many cars each family had by seeing how big the carports were; how many automatic laundries were owned by looking for clotheslines in backyards; how badly paint was peeling and how well weeds were taking over the lawns; how the housewives and children were dressed.

The Wrens paid particular attention to the general age level of their town, looking for toys in front yards and checking statistics at the chamber of commerce. They figured a "young" town, with many children to educate, would surely mean heavier school taxes over the years. They also made note of the town's public improvements—pavement, sewers, curbs, and gutters—in an effort to determine what future taxes might be in this department.

They went to the county health department to learn what diseases might be particularly prevalent in this area; to the regional weather-bureau office to learn what particular catastrophes of nature, such as hurricanes and floods, might strike here.

They went to the library of the local newspaper to study two specific matters in the newspaper's files. One was the society page, to determine how much the town went in for high society, such as debutante parties and symphony balls (a swirl they didn't want to move into); and what sort of social activities the townspeople engaged in—bridge, cookouts, cocktail parties, dinner parties, jackstones, or rook. The second check was the newspaper's want ads, to see who was giving or seeking jobs, how many there were on each side, and for how much per week. A local newspaper, according to Mr. Wren, is the finest mirror you can get on a town you are about to choose. They bought a six-month subscription to the paper, to be sent to them in New York.

Mr. Wren, who had been in the food processing business for thirty years, wanted a town that had some food processing plants around. He found a couple. He just might want to go back to work later on. At least he would like to have a few fellows about who could speak his language, instead of being like the fellow who moved from the furniture center of Grand Rapids, Michigan, into a California trailer park. He also spent much time checking fishing opportunities, which was one of his better mistakes. The nearby Gulf of Mexico would surely have a couple of fish in it. And if he thought fishing was to be a significant and continuing joy of his retirement, he hadn't questioned men who had retired before him and had thought the same thing.

The Wrens got from the chamber of commerce the names of the three top real-estate agencies in town, called on one of them, introduced themselves, and said they would be moving to the town in about seven months. They would want an apartment, preferably in this or that section of town, for a year, after which they intended to buy a home. They told the agency they would be in touch by mail as the time approached for retirement.

The Wrens checked airline service between Houston and the West Coast, and Houston and New York, where their two children lived, to make sure of quick contact with them. They then flew back home, listed their home with a real-estate agent for rent, two months after their retirement date.

One week after his retirement Mr. Wren flew to Texas to sign a lease for an apartment their real-estate agent there had written them about, spent a day measuring all the rooms so Mrs. Wren could know what would and wouldn't fit, then hurried back home to pack.

You don't have to do things as the Wrens did. But you'd be safer if you made their kind of investigation. Too many people choose a retirement town because they went there a couple of times on vacation or because there are pretty elm trees on Main Street.

You might as well know that when you come to choosing your retirement town, you will be strongly influenced by how that town looks from here, now, rather than how it will look from there, in two years. Whip this if you can.

Any retired man or woman planning to move to a new town had just as soon look admirable. Happy, prosperous, and heading down the open road to a glamorous paradise; they are tempted to choose a town that will present this sort of image to co-workers and old friends. That's the main reason so many retired people have chosen such an area as Santa Barbara, California—it sounds glamorous almost anywhere in the United States.

This works fine for the moment, with letters going back to friends in the old town, and everybody saying that "Old Joe" and "Miss Mary" are really plucking the stars.

But the enchantment doesn't last long. People back home have to get on with their business. As the gap your departure left is filled, former co-workers and friends return to their preoccupation with right now and right here. You become a fuzzy picture to them after a while. And no less, they become fuzzy to you. You, too, have business to get on with. You have a new town to conquer.

In the main, despite the affections of old friends that will last a lifetime, you will seldom think about the old town after a couple of years. And you will be quite uninterested in whether it thinks you have a glamorous retirement town. Just wait and see.

One final thing: Don't add a guest room to your home in the new town, in expectation that old friends will come visiting. Certainly they promised. They always do. But they're going in a different direction on their vacation next year, or they were dying to stop and see you when they drove through your town last week but just didn't have time.

An old friend will drop in from back home once in a while. And there will be, at first, a few people from the old town who stay overnight to avoid a motel bill. That's about the size of that.

51

~~~~~~~~

FOUR

CHOOSING YOUR RETIREMENT RESIDENCE

Retirement housing, as a rule, isn't.

Many things are called retirement housing: brick veneer shoe-boxes in suburbia, penthouses in Miami, sprawling real-estate promotions in Arizona, even old city hotels that have been run out of business by the rise of the motor inns.

Certain housing has been represented as retirement housing because electric outlets have been placed waist-high and shelves have been placed low enough to reach without a stepladder, both of which thirty-year-old housewives have been using all the time.

There will be no genuine retirement housing until more progress is made toward designing a house that has no steps, that has floors on which a foot cannot slip, no matter what, that has beds which can be automatically raised and lowered for getting in and out, and chairs with the same virtue.

Most important, retirement housing, to be that, must move toward designs that pacify the soul of a man who, for the first time, is staying home twenty-four hours a day. And it should be designed for his wife who must live with him for the same period.

Until such housing comes along, you must choose for your retirement an abode that was designed primarily for a working man and spouse or for a family, neither of which you are anymore. Or you must choose a straight-out old folks abode. There are seven choices:

1. Keep your present home.
2. Rent an apartment.
3. Build a dream house.
4. Sign into a residential hotel.
5. Buy a trailer and park it.
6. Buy into a retirement community.
7. Enter a retirement home.

You must face different decisions in each of the seven general areas of homes, and the information given here should help you make them intelligently.

1. KEEP YOUR PRESENT HOME. You will probably be happier in your retirement if you keep your present home. Not because it's good retirement housing, which very likely it isn't, but because emotional factors, financial factors, and your simple peace of mind often outweigh convenience.

Regarded strictly as housing, your present home is too big for your retirement. It was presumably acquired for the rearing of your family, which is now grown and gone. You don't need the space that is left behind, except to dust it. You don't need a second floor, which was necessitated by the extra bedrooms for the children. You need the task of cleaning second-floor windows and repairing second-floor gutters like you need a hole in your head.

Your taxes, insurance, and upkeep of the house will cost you as much on a pension as they did on a salary, and very probably more. This means that your housing will evade its share of the economy drive that falls on all other phases of your living as retirement comes.

You probably didn't buy your house recently. Most people owning a home at retirement time bought it at least ten or fifteen years ago. So it grows more obstinate and more expensive all the time. It is, in fact, older now and more expensive than at any time since you acquired it. You will have more time in retirement to do the repairs yourself, but you will find after a while that only about 10 percent of them are fun and the rest are a tiresome and frustrating nuisance.

Older widows who are left alone usually come to the conclusion that they must give up the family home because they can't maintain it themselves and are unable to find—or afford—workmen to help them. Retired men, as a rule, can manage by themselves.

A final shortcoming of the old family home as retirement housing is that it is playing a losing game. Neighborhoods, as a rule, go down, not up. So, if you have owned your home for fifteen years or so, it is well down the road toward that day when the area will be rezoned for apartments or for commercial buildings, or when a different character of residents will be moving in. This decline could happen to your housing anywhere, even to new retirement housing you bought. But in general a neighborhood can be assured of about twenty years before its seams begin to show.

All these factors should not necessarily lead you to sell your old home and find new shelter. As explained earlier, other factors are more important to some retired people than the mere housing qualities of their home. Usually they are happier when they stay on.

2. RENT AN APARTMENT. A rented apartment in a good building, in a good neighborhood, is probably the finest retirement housing you can find. Not necessarily the finest life, but the finest residence.

You pay your rent, keep the TV volume low, and figure out how to lure the janitor up from the basement to fix an occasional faucet leak—and that's it. All the mechanics of the housing burden are taken away. Painting, heating, yard work, roof repairs, broken windows, water mains, sewage disposal, garbage, real-estate taxes, assessments, screens, storm windows—all these become somebody else's problem. You just pay the rent. And keep the TV low.

A rented apartment is about the most flexible residence you can have. Normally, you will sign a one-year lease for it and renew it as long as you choose. Should an unexpected development come in your retirement—a spouse dies, or you need to move away to nurse one of your children, or you just become fed up and want to go—it doesn't have to become a federal case. You sublease the apartment, which sometimes you can do immediately, or you hold on until the lease expires and then go.

A rented apartment is one of the few areas in our society where the retired person is not only as good as but better than anybody else. At least to the landlord. The retired renter, presuming he chose an apartment his income can afford, is as reliable as a pension check. He or she asks no delay in paying the rent because of a strike, a layoff, or because he or she is fired. The retired tenant doesn't get a hurry-up transfer by the company to Rochester. That's all over now. Nor does he get a promotion to vice-president and suddenly become too good for the apartment.

The retired apartment tenant is stable, quiet, and opposed to arguments with other tenants. He doesn't clutter the apartment foyer with tricycles. He pays on time. Landlords love him.

Should you choose an apartment as your retirement residence, you should choose one if possible that is within walking distance of a city transportation route, a drugstore, and a supermarket. In time you may want to discard your car. You should choose an apartment that is on the first floor of a building or in a building with an elevator. Don't compromise on a second-floor apartment without an elevator by thinking one flight of stairs won't matter. Not now, maybe, but next year?

You will lose two important things by moving from your house into an apartment building. One will be access to a workshop and to a yard where you can grow flowers. The other will be the daily brush with the passing parade of life, such as newspaper boys, solicitors, strollers, garbage collectors, meter readers, and children. An apartment, especially in a large building is splendid isolation.

You must understand, too, that if you move from a family home to an apartment in the same town you are likely not to see much of the neighbors who called on you most. They would not choose to come into an apartment lobby in the clothes they wore to knock on your back door. And they aren't inclined to dress.

Something should be said here about cooperative apartments. They come in a variety of names now, but essentially they all work on about the same plan. Under this plan, you buy your apartment, at a figure usually somewhat below the price you would pay for a house of the same size. You then agree to pay your share of the cost of operating the apartment building. This is often called an assessment, is paid on the first of the month, and covers such things as taxes, heat, upkeep, and janitor services.

In most instances the owner-residents organize a committee or a board of directors to manage the operation and set the assessments, varying the assessments from time to time as operating costs change.

Many retired people have bought these co-op apartments. Some authorities in retirement housing recommend them. But before you buy, you might consider the following: Co-op apartments in many cities are quite difficult to unload, if you ever want to move; management boards in some of them would not allow you to rent your apartment to a nonowner.

The main value of a co-op apartment is that you "own" a piece of this particular building. Nobody can throw you out at the end of the year, as the landlord might if you were a renter. The question here is why would a landlord ever want to throw out a stable retired tenant who was paying his rent?

A second value of a co-op is that you and a group of your particular friends can all buy in together, and be assured you can always be neighbors—a good way, for instance, of providing a built-in bridge foursome. Maybe you'd like such in retirement. Maybe not.

3.   BUILD A DREAM HOUSE.

It takes a while to build a dream house. Maybe two years or so of choosing a lot, drawing blueprints, changing your mind, selecting colors, negotiating with contractors, choosing fixtures, changing your mind. For most people of retirement age it is like gulping from the fountain of youth.

So go on with the project if this has been your yen. You'll have so much fun out of it before you're through that you'll probably not mind too much the $5,000 you lose on the deal.

You will come out all right with it, if you use the conservatism that should be natural to your age, and if you make reasonable note of the information given here.

You will probably choose an outlying area for your dream home, since very few lots for that sort of thing are left toward the center of town. You will choose a wild and wooly lot carved out of somebody's farm, in which case you will have difficulties getting water, sewer lines, gas lines, electric lines, and telephone. Or you will choose a lot in a suburban development where city services are all assured.

You'll probably favor the latter. Keep in mind that most other people will, too, and that many of them will be young families with school-age children. This means you'll be paying taxes through the years building schools for the kiddies and biting your tongue as they chase balls through your flower garden.

Even so, you will have neighbors, most of whom you'll like, and there will always be somebody close by to call in case of emergency. The isolated lot, with its peace and quiet, sounds good. But it's too lonely to wear well.

You will presumably be acquiring your last house, which means you will be growing old here. Make sure the location is one that will have public transportation when the time comes that you don't want to drive your car. Make sure a shopping center will be reachable. See if it might be a possible place for the survivor to live on alone if the husband or wife dies.

Any suburban housing development these days provides many types of easy mortgage terms. Which is good. But before you buy a lot and build, make sure the mortgage terms aren't too easy. As a rule, the developments where people can buy a house and lot with virtually nothing down and two generations to pay don't last very well. Things get tough in a family, it has only a few dollars invested in the place, so it ups and moves out. This makes for a transient neighborhood, with steadily declining values.

By the way, you can nearly always get a clue as to the type of neighbors you will have in a suburban development where you buy your lot. Make an auto tour in a five-mile radius of the development. If you find an automobile assembly plant, you'll have a lot of auto workers around. If you find a tall insurance building, you'll have typists and clerks. If an airport, a couple of pilots and a lot of ground crewmen.

Suburban developers now have frequently spotted a couple of large, well-established industries near the land they buy. These are prime sources of customers.

The house you build on your lot will be fairly conventional in design. You hadn't intended it that way, since it's a dream house, but you find that every unconventional thing you wanted costs money. And the compromises aren't too bad. It's still all yours and all new.

A contractor will build your house, since people seldom employ architects for houses under $40,000. The contractor will have been checked out carefully, and is presumably honorable. He will need some money as soon as he starts work, which is sometimes a shock to a retired couple building their first house. They had expected to pay him when the job was done. But the contractor needs materials, and he won't finance their purchase over the period required to build the house.

If you intend to pay for the new house with proceeds from the sale of your old one and you haven't sold it yet, you can make arrangements at the bank for a loan fund which the contractor can draw on.

You will have a written agreement with the contractor, providing an exact price for the job, and a date on which the job will be finished. You will beware of any cost-plus deal with him, since this allows you to pay for any mistakes he makes.

You will let a lawyer review the agreement before you sign it, making sure among other things that the contractor can deliver.

If you have the money, and presumably you will when your old house is sold, pay for the new house and be done with it. You don't want to bother with mortgage payments in retirement. You also don't want to be a patsy. Any money you have will probably go into a savings and loan account at 4½ percent return. A mortgage, when all the fees are in, may run you up to 9 percent.

The information here hits only a few high spots. Go to your public library and borrow some of the many books there on building dream houses. You'll learn something, but also these books will be one more delightful ingredient in the adventure you're cooking up.

4. SIGN INTO A RESIDENTIAL HOTEL. Some of the most elegant residences in the world—penthouses on Lake Shore Drive or garden suites overlooking the Pacific—are residential hotels for retired people. Also, some of the most deplorable residences in the world—grimy cells in three-floor walk-ups or smelly hovels in city slums—are residential hotels for retired people.

So you have quite a choice.

You will choose a residential hotel, if that is your wish for retirement, on the basis of a dollar bill. The more you pay, the better you get. There is virtually no other consideration in the matter.

In some ways the residential hotels have the great virtue of the rented apartments: Pay your rent and keep the TV low, and all the mechanics of housing are taken off your hands. You do not have kitchen facilities, as a rule, which is bad for a budget. You have given up your furniture and most of your personal treasures, since residential hotels are furnished, and this leaves a hollowness in in your life.

Too, residential hotels, except those in the luxury class, are often located in commercial sections of a city where the sidewalk is your front yard and rooftops are your view.

If you have the courage to go and look—and why not, since all they can do is throw you out?—stroll into the lobbies of some of the better residential hotels in the cities and resorts you visit on your next vacation. You will see gracious old ladies sitting around in the easy chairs, doing nothing. You will see a few old gentlemen strolling around, doing nothing. Now and then you will notice that they go to the elevator, to return to their rooms, to do nothing there for a while, then return to the lobby to do nothing. The curse of these well-to-do is that they feel they must maintain dignity, must never show they want or need anything. To make gestures of friendship toward others, or to show any aggressiveness in developing activities for themselves, would reveal a hunger in themselves they do not wish to reveal.

The most useless and perhaps the most miserable of America's retired people are the well-to-do living in fine residential hotels.

By contrast, poor residential hotels are often bubbling with life. The retired here frequently share rooms, congregate on the front porch or sidewalk in the evening to talk or play games, often have arranged to have their meals together in nearby cafés. There is comradeship among the poor in these hotels. It thins out as you go up the economic ladder.

More than normal caution should be taken by those preparing to move into a residential hotel in these times, particularly those below the luxury class. The rise of the motels and motor inns has been rough on commercial hotels in the city, and real-estate promoters have been converting many of them into retirement homes or residential quarters for older people. This is well and good, except that some of these commercial hotels were never very desirable buildings in the first place, and others have become so dilapidated in the recent years of hard times that they are not particularly fit places for older people.

One commercial hotel recently closed down because it could no longer meet the city's fire safety regulations. A short time later it was announced the hotel would become a retirement home. Were the fire dangers corrected? Or were the fire standards for a retirement home not so high as for a hotel? You have to investigate to know.

5. BUY A TRAILER AND PARK IT. No matter what your prejudices have been, no matter what awful things people have told you, sooner or later you should take a good, hard look at the idea of living in a trailer, or mobile home, or whatever they call it.

Romance, adventure, and economy are all tied up with trailer living—all the way from the dream of bouncing down the open road with a curtained bug hitched to the car, to the palatial four-roomers parked by a Florida beach with an awning out front.

Many retired people have been, and are, fascinated by the whole thing.

You may be, too. Or you may be repelled. But you should have a look.

Trailer living, until recent times, has been considered by many as a not very nice way to live. Trailer dealers will heatedly dispute this, and people who have been living in trailers are inclined to throw rocks at you if you say it. But the fact is that no prominent lady in your town would have ever condescended to retire into a trailer—no, sir! No matter what her husband said.

This is changing. You can now find important and socially prominent retired couples living in trailers in parts of Florida and California. Not everywhere, you understand, but in beautiful chosen trailer parks, and in trailers that have been designed for luxury living.

Over recent years, trailer parks, which is where the trailers go to sit, have been considered by many people to be not very nice neighborhoods. People living in such parks will throw rocks at you for saying this, too. Trailer parks, from World War II on, attracted all kinds of people. Transient workers, married students, people without means, people from depressed areas, undesirables —all kinds of people. With wash hanging out to dry, unkempt children running about, and frequent signs of civic irresponsibility, the parks got a bad name. But these parks, which everybody saw, were adjuncts to city life—cheap housing for people struggling to hold on in a city. They weren't the retirement trailer parks which have always been a different breed of animal and have usually been located in the smaller towns of the sunshine states rather than in the junky outskirts of a city.

The neighborhood life afforded by the better retirement parks now is as good and as desirable as you would find on the normal suburban street in New Jersey or Michigan. Again, not all the parks, but the better ones.

With these matters out of the way—and it is important that you know that stigmas, once prevalent, are fading—the most important factor about trailer living for most retired people is the economy. You can buy a secondhand trailer that is adequate for a retired couple and looks decent enough for you not to be ashamed of it, for about $4,000 and up. But suppose you do a little better than that—you pay $7,500. The house you have owned is worth $15,000. You save about $28 a month right off, because the $15,000 house has been costing you about $56 a month just sitting there. (The $15,000 tied up could have been giving you a 4 percent return or better in investment.)

Your taxes on the trailer residence would normally be far below what they were on a $15,000 house. But if you move the trailer into a state that has a homestead exemption law or that taxes trailers as vehicles instead of houses, you have it made.

You will have insurance to pay and some personal property taxes, but both will be less than in the house. You will have some upkeep costs, but metal predominates on most trailers and the costs are low.

You will have to pay somebody a fee for the right to park your trailer on his property. You can choose the side of a ravine on some farmer's lower forty for maybe ten dollars a month, and get nothing but a place to park. You can choose one of the well-developed trailer parks where you will have sewer, light, and water connections, neighbors, nearby markets, and police protection. The fee will range, as a rule, from forty to eighty dollars a month.

From the early 1960's on, the Mobile Homes Manufacturers Association, leading trade organization of the trailer builders, has been strongly promoting the development of fine trailer parks. Some now have park laundries, movies, entertainment, gas and oil, and markets for most of your needs.

Before you choose a park, measure its mileage from downtown, from the doctor's office, from your church, and wherever else you will be going regularly. Some of the new parks are beautiful, luxurious, and delightful . . . and twenty miles from nowhere.

You will probably buy a trailer, if you buy one, that won't do much trailing. One that is large enough for comfortable living is a cumbersome thing. And while the average driver can manage one on the highway after a little practice, it may take a truck engine to do it. And it's work. Frequently people buy their trailer near the scene where they'll park it, or actually in the park where some couple is giving it up. Increasingly, they are putting permanent foundations underneath, and staying put.

The ingenuity that is going into the design of the new trailers has magic to it, and only by going into a dealer's yard and looking can you appreciate it. Nearly everything is built in, including range, refrigerator, beds, and sofas. Housekeeping just almost isn't.

Now, nothing that is said here is intended to encourage you to go buy a trailer. There are things about such a life that aren't good. Go take a look, weigh the pros and cons, and make up your mind. You should consider, for sure, that when you retire into a trailer you give up most of the personal possessions you've had at home. No four-poster beds, for instance. No favorite chairs, tables, rugs, or china cabinets. But maybe a vase or two. And a picture. You must consider, also, that you're going to have to love your spouse, because these quarters are going to be the closest you have ever had. Unless you've tried a Pullman berth. Togetherness is the new order of things, and even though partitions are built between the rooms, a couple lives as one in a trailer.

Then there is the matter of a garden to putter in—there usually isn't one. And no basement. And no tool shop. And not a great deal to do with all the time that has been saved from the housework.

Still, people by the thousands have considered and accepted the shortcomings of trailer life. Many have doubled their commitment to it by buying one trailer they leave permanently in the South and a second one they leave permanently back in the old hometown, then commuting back and forth with the seasons.

In the trailer parks of Arizona, California, and Florida you can frequently rent a trailer home for a year or for the summer season when the owner goes back North. You may want to get a tenant for your home for a year and sample trailer life before you buy it.

6. BUY INTO A RETIREMENT COMMUNITY.   Be careful about retirement communities. Are you buying a genuine community

for retired people? Or are you buying a real-estate promotion?

During recent years many fabulous housing projects have been erected all the way from the desert sands of Arizona to the lagoons of Florida and are called retirement settlements. Some started out to be that, and remained that. Some started out to be that, found customers scarce, and lowered the age levels to the tricycle set. Some apparently never intended anything except to make a hurry-up dollar on real estate.

You can find many housing variations in these developments, most of them modern and nearly all of them appealing. Built-in appliances and convenience are the keynote of all developments, but you will rarely find any drastic departures from the conventional housing now being built. A ramp here and there, close-by shopping facilities, occasional community recreation facilities, often a swimming pool. It's nice living, but nothing that leans very strongly to specialty housing for a seventy-four-year-old arthritic.

Maybe you'll like what you see. Maybe you'll want to buy. Just understand what it is, actually, that you're buying.

In the developments you will find separate houses, row houses, apartments, duplexes, the works. Financial arrangements are about as varied. You can rent, or you can buy. You can make various types of mortgage deals. You can make arrangements for various types of lifetime occupancy, with the property reverting to the owner on your death. The style of the residences and the manner of financing change from one development to the other.

Some fine corporations have been involved in developing the communities that are called retirement settlements. They have constructed fine residences in many cases and have advertised them well. As a result, they have attracted some good people. So in the better projects you might expect to find a banker from Iowa or an Ivy League professor as your neighbor. You might expect to find a good many gray hairs and bald heads about, since this advertising message has been directed mainly toward retired people.

You may find children around. Some of the projects started out accepting only genuine retired people of age sixty-five or so, then cut the age limit to about sixty-two, then fifty-five, then fifty-two, and so on. But children aren't bad to have around. They keep you from feeling that you have been isolated from society in a ghetto of old folks.

7. ENTER A RETIREMENT HOME. In general, retirement homes have come to mean a haven for retired people who have become incapable, physically or mentally, to cope with the outside world. Or for those who just don't want to bother with the mechanics of coping.

This is not always the case. There are retired people at age sixty-six or so, still hale and hearty, who prefer to move into the tranquillity of a retirement home where their daily needs can be met. There are normally professional staffs to handle any health problems that may arise.

Retirement homes, like other retirement residences, come in many flavors. There are commercial homes, usually in and around cities, that are operated by doctors or nurses or others for a profit. City governments usually make an effort to license and inspect these commercial homes, not always with good results. Now and then a scandalous story about one of them appears in the newspaper.

These commercial homes—not always but often—are depositories for old parents which children don't want around anymore. The old parent doesn't have the proper modern manners, has developed undesirable habits, interferes with the social progress of the ambitous children, so the children find it practical to pay the retirement-home fee and move the old parent out. "For their own good," of course.

You may find a commercial retirement home that is as fine as a Boy Scout oath. Just be sure to look in the closets.

Some of the finest of retirement homes are operated by religious groups. Their only mission in life is to take care of you. Most of the well-known religious denominations now have homes in operation, and most of them have waiting lists. The pastor of your church can usually guide you in a selection.

Along with the church homes are those operated by fraternal organizations and by labor unions. As a rule these two groups cater somewhat more to their own members than do the church groups. Their only mission, also, is to take care of you.

The better retirement homes are about the closest approach in the country to actual "retirement housing." The ramps, the electric plugs, the low shelves, are all there, but at almost every turn in such a home is some cleverness that has been installed for the specialized needs of older people. There will be a dining table, for instance, with a notch in it to accommodate a resident in a wheelchair. There will be two types of matting running alongside each other in the hall, one for the sure-of-foot, one for the unsure. There will be a clinic down the hall. There will be a wing for residents who no longer live with reality.

On this side of the wheelchair, the unsure foot, and the special wing, there are facilities in most of the homes for those who are still alert and active. Workshops in the basement, sun-rooms with television, sewing rooms, hobby shops, and that sort of thing. There is usually a fairly full schedule of special events that includes movies, visiting musical groups, speakers, and religious activities.

Retirement homes of the better type are about the only place in our society where older people are the most important thing in sight. Unless it's a Social Security office or a factory where they make arthritis pills. The staffs of the homes are trained to care for the particular needs of the later years, and the people who join these staffs seem invariably to have affection for the old. With their training, there would be better jobs if they wanted them.

Should you start making plans to enter a retirement home? Well, probably not yet. But keep your eye on one. If infirmities come or if the luster of life in the outside world fades, you will have warning. Maybe a year or so. Then you can act, if in the meantime you have spotted a home you might like and have made some inquiries.

The financial arrangements on entering a retirement home will confuse you, because they are many and varied. Some are straightaway rental plans—so much per month as long as you stay. Some are straightaway purchase plans—an advance payment for life care. There are many plans in between, including some where you surrender all your assets, including Social Security benefits, and in return get lifetime care; others where you pay, say, $10,000 in advance, then small monthly payments for life. Nearly all plans provide for room, board, laundry, and some form of medical care.

Home with the Children

The seven areas of retirement residences described here pretty well cover the field. But there is one other area, and if you are like most retired people, you will be tempted at some point to try it.

It is a residence in the home of one of your children.

You will move in with your children, if you do, for one of three primary reasons: (1) you don't have the resources to do anything else, (2) you are talked into the idea that two families can live cheaper under one roof than one, or (3) you just like the idea.

If you have to, you have to. So not too much can be said about that. But if there is a choice, give some serious thinking to what follows.

ONE. Retired people who move into their children's home are usually not very happy. You won't be told this on television, you won't hear it anywhere, because people who once make the mistake—like those who move inadvisedly to Florida—can find no easy way to retreat. And they won't admit they are unhappy.

The cliché about two women in the same kitchen is a factor in the unhappiness of these situations, but not a decisive one. The trouble comes mainly from the fact that the retired parents soon begin to feel hampered all across the household board. They don't feel free to sit in the living room as they always have, or eat the same way, or watch TV and read the papers the same way, go to bed and get up the same way. They strive to please, to adjust to what they soon realize is a child-centered home and a new generation. You will notice, if you watch one of these situations, that the retired parents will in time increasingly seek the seclusion of their bedroom and the outdoors.

TWO. Financial arrangements which parents make to move

into a child's home are seldom beneficial to them and are often disastrous. A common arrangement is for the parents to put up the cash for the down payment on a home the child wants, with the child taking over the mortgage payments and providing a lifetime home for the parents. What happens if the child, or his or her spouse, loses a job and can't meet the mortgage payments? Another common arrangement is for the parents and child to go fifty-fifty on the cost of the house and the upkeep. Again, what happens if the child can't keep up?

Barring these calamities, there is always a possibility that the child will have to move out of town. A man who is going anywhere in business today, particularly if he is with a large corporation, is frequently transferred every few years to a new town. Or if the man changes companies to get ahead, he often must try a new town for a new job. Again this leaves the older parents who have a joint financial arrangement sitting there holding the bag.

And they are dealing with their flesh and blood, not with a hardheaded business partner. They can't bring themselves to force a hard business deal with a child who must break up the house partnership. They certainly wouldn't want to hold the child back. So they take over the whole obligation and manage as best they can.

Deeds to property in which retired parents and their child have joint rights are always a sticky business. The child dies, and his or her spouse remarries. Or there is a divorce. Or the child becomes liable for a large debt, and the child's part of the house is seized to satisfy the claim.

If the retired parents contribute money to the child's house, having no claim in the deed and no written agreement—and many parents would think it crass to ask either—all sorts of dire developments can come if a break occurs in the child's own domestic life.

THREE. Parents have found, in practice, that when they take up residence in the home of a child they become particularly vulnerable to money requests from the child's family. Financial crises come constantly to young families, and the parents find it uncomfortable to sit by when a donation of a hundred dollars of their savings would solve the crisis. Especially when they're in the next room. They find it uncomfortable, too, when the child's family wants a new car, or a vacation trip to Yellowstone, or a new sofa—and they want loudly and strongly—while Mom and Pop are sitting on savings they'll never use anyway.

Children are people first and children second. All retired parents with a little money must realize that if they have more than one child, and choose to move in with only one, the others will be a little suspicious.

If you have now given some thinking to these warning signals against moving in with your children, think for a while how delightful it will be to be in the house with people who after all are the most precious in the world to you. Where else can you see your grandchildren all day long? Who else would console you when you're blue and take care of you when you're ill?

Add up the pros and cons, close your ears to entreaties of everybody, and make up your own gray-haired mind.

FIVE

MAKING YOUR WIFE HAPPY IN RETIREMENT

The "Wonderful Me" concept you have when you go home in retirement is probably the most exclusive concept on earth. Nobody—nobody at all—has it but you.

The wife waiting at home for you, though she adores you, though she is ready now to give you for the rest of her life the tender loving care you so richly deserve, is not going to be too happy. She is not going to think that your coming home to stay is the most joyous thing that ever happened. She may say it is. She may profess how happy she is. She may join the chorus of the "Wonderful Me" you are singing.

Then she may slip off to the attic and cry.

Now pick yourself up off the floor and dust yourself off. The words above say just what you thought they said. Read them again. Believe them. They are true.

You are coming home to live for twenty-four hours a day in what is essentially the castle of your wife. It may well bring into her personal life the greatest crisis she has faced.

Give it five minutes of thinking and you can understand why. You are invading her jobs, no less than if somebody had come to your company to look over your shoulder eight hours a day. For maybe forty years she has run the house, cleaned the floors, cooked the meals, dealt with the milkman, bribed the men who collect the garbage. This is her job, her life, as your job to a large extent has been your life. Now you come home in retirement and she gets somebody to tell her how to do it.

Your wife has had about 100,000 hours to herself since she married you, presuming you have been married for forty years. In all these hours she has had to find something to do. Among this something have been daytime friends, usually women such as herself whose menfolk were away on a job. The husbands of all these friends don't retire at the same time you do.

So? So your wife feels an obligation to stay home and keep you company, or to keep women friends from visiting the house and getting in your hair, and thus lets friends she had made over the years begin fading away, along with the afternoon social functions, the clubs, the morning coffees, the organizations you always thought were silly anyway.

And in these 100,000 hours your wife has been doing the mysterious things wives do when left alone in their homes. Making cookies for neighborhood kiddies? Sitting before television watching the soap operas? Taking naps? Reading movie magazines? Looking out the window and dreaming? Patching a hole in the mattress or darning your socks or doing the laundry or sewing buttons on or disinfecting the bathroom or some of a multitude of other inconspicuous household chores that you have taken for granted and didn't know were done? Much of this must now be dropped or modified, or else she must have an explanation for you of why she is taking so much time with things instead of with you.

Your ego is probably bleeding by now. But read on. Some patches are coming. These preliminaries have been necessary in order that you get a correct perspective of just what the situation is when you come home in retirement. Only with an honest perspective can you succeed in "Making Your Wife Happy in Retirement." Only by making her happy can you be happy.

Now there are all sorts of wives, naturally. Every man who is reading this will be sure his wife is a special case, which indeed she may be—a battle-ax, a spendthrift, a living doll, a sweetheart. But there is one common denominator of the wives of almost all men who retire: Somehow, and in their strange way, they love their man. They simply could not have lived with a man until age sixty-five without loving him, because there is nothing on earth more difficult to live with than a man.

So, in return for this love—whether it shows or not—set out to make your wife happy in retirement. But if you want to be obstinate about it, set out to make her happy anyway because only in this way will you reap the fulfillment that can be yours in the freedom you are getting. Honest. Just wait and see. Your wife may have been difficult over these last ten or fifteen years. You're in for an education in difficulty if—with the woes you are now bringing home to your wife—you fail to initiate some positive steps toward compatibilty and oneness.

After all, you're going to be like a little boy rattling around the house for a year or so. You want to be petted, don't you? And get some cookies?

The technique of making a wife happy in retirement will include such things as a bottle of perfume occasionally, going somewhere she wants to go for once instead of fishing, and a couple of comments on how lovely she looks this morning. But in the main it will be the more basic, the more prosaic, things that matter.

The things that matter fall into three departments: preparing your wife, helping your wife, and protecting your wife.

Handle these three departments well and you will have with your wife the compatibility and trust that will make retirement good. You will have the satisfaction of knowing you have shown nobility to the woman who plighted her troth to you. And someday, you may even get fresh flowers on your grave a couple of times a year.

Preparing Your Wife

In many companies and institutions a man hears his first small sound of retirement about six years before he reaches sixty-five.

In another year, or on his sixtieth birthday, he hears that he will have to make a decision on one of the options in his pension plan. He will have to decide whether he will want his full pension to come to him, starting one month after he retires, or whether he will want to take only a part of the pension due him and leave the remainder to provide a pension for his wife after he dies.

Not all pension plans have this option, but many do. In many cases, if they do, the man must make the decision at age sixty and then stick by it.

From this point until the farewell party at sixty-five the sounds of retirement will grow louder and more frequent. A good man should see that his wife hears every one of them. Because they are her business no less than his. That's right. While the job has been his sovereign domain, or so he has contended, and the company has been his private possession, or so he has contended, the issue at hand is retirement, which is an extension of the job and company, and an extension in which the wife will be immersed up to her neck.

The better employers, probably including your own, bite their fingernails over this. They know retirement is the business of the wife as well as of the employee. They know that the employee is going to be happier in retirement if his wife is acquainted with what the employer can, or can't, do about retirement.

But they dare not invade the employee's privacy, knowing that the employee, being a male animal, would resent it. They make veiled hints that perhaps the man should call his wife in for some of the retirement counseling sessions the employers try to hold, that the wife should be told what the pension will be, why it will be that, what other benefits go with it. But they dare only to hint.

So in preparing your wife for your retirement, do what professionals the employer has hired to understand such matters know you should do, and what your wife would like for you to do: Let her get in on the act.

By the time most of you read this, the limit on deciding to defer part of your pension for your wife may have passed. You signed that funny little paper on the lunch hour one day. Remember? Maybe at this point you can do nothing more about it. But talk it over with your wife, and if it seems advisable to the two of you that some sort of deferred payments on the pension should be made, go to the employer's personnel officer and see what you can do.

This is a starter. Now explain to your wife the ABC's of your pension, telling her what it will be, why, when it will start, how long it will continue. Then explain to her what other benefits, if any, you will get from the employer, such as paid-up life and health insurance.

Finally, when the employer has a retirement counseling class, or when the personnel office says it would like for you to drop by next week and discuss your retirement—and you are told your wife is invited, too—let your wife know she is invited, too. And let her come. Remember this is not your job they're talking about, which both the company and wife realize is your business. It is retirement, which is very much going to be the wife's business, too.

Take your wife with you to the Social Security office when you go to find out what your benefits will be.

Let her learn, for herself, that if she will be age sixty-two or older when you retire—and the two of you decide she should start collecting her benefits then—she can have the Social Security checks that are due her sent to her in her own name.

Insist that she get them in her own name. She is probably going to endorse them and turn them over to you anyway. But it will do her heart good, and she will see that you get some extra cookies, if she starts getting a check made out to her for maybe the first time in forty years.

It would be good of you to tell your wife just what retirement will mean to the personal budget you have been getting all these years. You won't need so much money from now on. The smokes, and a beer now and then. And a few coins to jingle. That's about all.

It would be good of you also to tell your wife gently that retirement will bring a change in whatever loot you have been getting on the job. You aren't going to get any from now on. The gifts at Christmas and the turkey on Thanksgiving if you have been an executive with clout, a purchasing agent, or some such. The donations from your staff or work crew, if you have been a boss. The free banquet tickets to the annual meeting of the Credit Union which you served as vice-president. And maybe a circus pass once in a while.

You are now on the road to preparing your wife for your retirement and making her happy. You had better get down to a few grim details.

Retirement is not a time for dying, necessarily. Any annuity company will provide you with statistics showing you'll be around quite a while yet. But retirement is a dramatic milestone in your life and will probably be the last one. It is the occasion to act on certain death-connected decisions. If you don't there will be no other milestone to remind you, and you will let the decisions slide.

You should make a will that will protect your wife after you do die, and she should make one that will protect you. Again, not because you are about to die but because if you don't use retirement as the excuse to make a will, you will have no other. Lawyers will make wills for from twenty-five dollars up each, and there is no other sure way to assure that your money will be channeled to your wife.

With the will out of the way, decide where you will want to be buried, when that time eventually comes. Go choose a cemetery lot in that location, pay for it, file the deed away, and forget the matter. You don't want your wife burying you in the backyard, do you? Well, she just may do that if she has to decide such an issue while in grief over you.

In selecting the place where you would like to be buried, you might refrain from being shortsighted. Many people are. You might ponder, for instance, the matter of just what you want for your grave. If you want it to be a continuation of your family history, a holding-hands with your youth, then the hilltop cemetery in the old hometown is probably for you. But if your wife wants the same thing and she came from another county, you've got a slight problem.

If, on the other hand, you want your grave to be a shrine for your children, for the friends around you, and if you'd like some flowers on it occasionally or would like loved ones to visit it, you had better pick a site the loved ones can get to on a Sunday afternoon. There are many retired people who have chosen to be buried back in an old hometown, and whose graves are visited by about three people in five years. Even loved ones in these times don't travel far to visit cemeteries.

One important note: Go to a well-established funeral home with your wife, make arrangements in writing for exactly the kind of funeral arrangements you both want, file the contract away with your family papers, and forget that matter, too. A time of grief is no time for either a husband or a wife to make funeral arrangements.

Your wife, at this point, is going to begin thinking you care. She's going to be convinced of it when you take your next step.

That step is to call a husband-wife conference for some evening, prepare to give about two hours to it, and get comfortable on the living-room sofa. You want to move to another state when you retire. Or you want to build a retirement cottage in the suburbs. Or you want to exchange your house for an apartment. Or in some other way you want to make a change in the way you have been living. This is well and good, but explain to your wife that before any such change can be carried out the two of you must determine whether the changed way of life will be a fit life for the wife in case the husband dies. And once more it is not that retirement is a time for dying but a matter of making such decisions at this time or letting them go by default.

Normally, husbands die before their wives do, meaning that the wife will have several years of widowhood. And probably aloneness. This can be deadly and frightening for a widow. For instance, the couple that builds a retirement hideaway in the country may have a delightful life as long as the husband is around to protect, to fix, and to drive the car, but a nightmare for the widow if he goes. The couple moving far away to the sunshine may have a life in which, together, they have happiness, but in which, if one were left to live it alone, there would be only misery.

So analyze these things in depth with your wife. If you plan any sort of change, make your wife think through the problems she might have if left alone, and make her tell you her solutions.

If, instead of moving, you own your home and decide you will live on in it, you'd better climb up tomorrow and have a look at the shingles. By retirement time a husband should begin putting in good repair, for the long pull, any house where his widow must live. She can't replace shingles, and you may not be able to leave her enough money to pay for this—even if she could find somebody to do the job, which she probably couldn't.

Finally, in preparing your wife for happiness in your retirement, prepare her for *you*. If it is your intention to come home and be a heel, expecting her to wait on you, tell her. If you plan to turn the basement into a workshop and leave it looking as if a storm came through, tell her. If you plan to sleep every morning until ten o'clock, tell her. If you plan to fish every day and expect her to clean the fish, if any, tell her.

A wife is a remarkably adjustable creature. She can adjust to almost anything, as she will show you when she adjusts just to your being home twenty-four hours a day. Warn her of any special ways in which you plan to mess up her home and her life, and she will prepare for them.

On the other hand, if you intend to come home as a good guy, let your wife know. She would welcome any specific details as to just how you propose to be a good guy. You might give a few evenings of thinking to these details, then pass on your conclusions to her. You will continue to get up at the same time every morning, except that two evenings a week there are late movies on TV which you'd like for her to stay up with you to watch, and on the mornings afterward you'd like to sleep an hour later. You will want the same kind of breakfast you've been getting, and the same kind of dinner, but you'd like a little lunch, too, and a can of soup might handle that—you'd know how to heat it. You will want to fish and play golf but you'll make it a point always to let her know a day in advance so she can make her own plans.

You get the idea. Outline to her what design of living you are expecting. It will prepare her better than anything else.

Helping Your Wife

There are those husbands who believe that, no matter what, wives should do all the work that is done in the house. Except for fixing a light socket, maybe. If you are one of these, you'd better just not read what is about to be said next. Use the time to hunt yourself a couple of playmates because you're going to need them.

A wife has the same right to retire that a man has. Figure it on a legal or moral basis, or just on common justice, and you will find it difficult to come to any other conclusion.

But, obviously, somebody still must cook and make the beds. And, at last reports, nobody was running around giving pensions to housewives. So you should find some sort of compromise on the housework that will enable both you and your wife to keep your pride and share the chores.

In the main, it is better that the chores be divided in such a way that each works, and finishes, about the same time. This prevents one from annoying the other, but it also provides opportunity for the togetherness that makes a good retirement. Playmates, except for each other, aren't too plentiful for either the husband or the wife in retirement. With the work scheduled carefully, the husband and wife are their own companions.

Many varieties of work schedules can be set up. The one you adopt should be based on your particular talents and on the personalities of each of you. The one here is for a normal day and is offered only as a guide. Modify it to fit your tastes.

Work Schedule

Arise together. Nothing throws retirement compatibility out of tune more quickly than different sleeping habits. When one stays up late and sleeps late or when one takes naps and the other doesn't, a day of togetherness never gets in step.

79

Wife	*Husband*
Cooks breakfast	Sets the table, empties dishwasher, serves the fruit juice, fills the cream pitcher, gets the newspaper
Makes the bed, cleans bedroom and bath	Cleans up the kitchen and puts things in the dishwasher
Cleans the living room	Takes out garbage and trash
Gathers up the laundry and irons yesterday's wash	Does the laundry. If there is no dryer he does *not* hang out clothes in the backyard

There are certain chores in the house that are not fitting for a man to do, such as hanging clothes on a line where neighbors can see him. In general, the man's household chores should be out of the neighbor's sight.

Prepare lunch and clean up kitchen together.

Wife	*Husband*
Sews, mends, beautifies her house	Does the yard work
Cooks dinner	Does needed minor repairs in the house, sets the table

Clean up the kitchen together, and go into the living room together to relax.

Retired husbands and wives seem happier when they do the marketing together, and when they go on shopping excursions together. A work schedule that allows it, but that allows a certain amount of time each day to be alone and pursue personal ends, is nearly always best.

Many husbands coming home in retirement spend several days sizing up the domicile, and then get an itch to tell their wives how they can improve certain things they are doing. They see cobwebs the wife hasn't seen for seven years. They figure out a quicker way to make a bed, a better way to run a vacuum cleaner. And during the commercials while they're sitting watching daytime TV they get some brilliant ideas on rearranging the furniture.

These are not exactly what was meant for "making your wife happy in retirement."

Neither is the yen of the newly retired husband to tell his wife what to do about her kitchen. His organized mind—organized because he spent so many years on a job—cries out against the arrangement of the pantry and the way the pots and pans are stored. He'll fix 'em.

He tackles the chaos in the pantry and starts organizing certain types of food on certain shelves so somebody can make sense of the mess and find things. Whereupon his wife, who has had the chaos organized just as she liked it and could find what she wanted in the dark, is herself now thrown into chaos.

It's the same with the pots and pans. There has never yet been a retired man who didn't think he could make more sense out of the manner in which his wife dumps them in cupboards and out of sight. But the wife knows where what is in the dump, and how to find a skillet to fry an egg in. She doesn't after her husband reorganizes.

Any man who desires to help his wife with the household when he retires should keep his cotton-picking hands off her organization of her kitchen. It doesn't help her. Furthermore, it usually makes him look a little silly because his wife knew all the time a pantry can't be organized, and pots and pans can't be arranged to look neat.

It is this sort of thing that makes a retired man lose face when he comes home and makes his wife entertain her first bit of doubt whether he is really as brilliant as she always thought he was.

It is a fairly well established part of our culture that a wife bosses the kitchen of her home. A retired husband would be most helpful to his wife if he refrained from challenging this. If he wants to cook now and then, she'll let him. And clean up the mess

81

he makes. If he wants to broil the steaks tomorrow night, fine. Or suggests he would like to prepare spaghetti with garlic sauce on Sunday.

Just stop it there, and let the wife be boss of the kitchen.

The wife also, by tradition, is manager of the household maintenance. She knows how to do the job considerably better than a husband who has been off for forty years on a job while she did it. So the retired husband who uses some of the gray-haired wisdom he didn't use on the pantry or the pots and pans, and lets his wife set the pattern for what household chores they will share, will be helping her no end. Indeed.

Protecting Your Wife

A man by age sixty-five normally has in his head a large amount of information that will be vital in the protection of his wife in her later years, if he will pass it along to her. It is mostly financial and legal information, and since man is the kind of creature he is, he has not been willing, or has not bothered, to do it.

As pointed out earlier, you would be a devoted husband if you brought your wife in on all retirement information given you by the employer; if you did not move her to some location where she would be miserable if you left her a widow; and if you did not leave her a dilapidated house. The suggestions that follow now are in that vein.

• Explain to your wife what joint ownership of a house means, if you have a home in joint ownership. There are different kinds of joint ownership, you know. Some of them *in some states* provide that a home will pass automatically to the wife if the husband dies. Some do not. Tell your wife whether your house would pass automatically to her (you probably don't know and had better ask a lawyer), and if it wouldn't what steps she would take to get full possession. And what inheritance taxes on your half of the house she would have to pay. Some men at retirement who love their wives—and trust them—have switched their homes from their own names, or from joint names, into the exclusive name of the wife. Not so much to avoid taxes as to protect their wives from the expense and bother of getting the title changed.

• Explain to your wife that, if you should die, she very probably could not cash any checks that are coming to you—pension, Social Security, veteran benefits, etc. At least she couldn't until she made a federal case out of it. Explain to her also that *in some states* everything the two of you have in joint ownership, such as house, stocks, bonds, safety box, bank accounts, can be frozen if you should die, and remain frozen until tax appraisers come to size up the estate. These two factors mean that if you should die suddenly while you wife had only $2.85 in the house, that $2.85 might be all she could get her hands on until long after you were buried. A way to avoid such a crisis, if you love your wife, is to set up some part of the family assets in her name exclusively. A $500 savings account would do it. Full title to the house would do it since she could borrow emergency funds with the title. Full ownership of stocks or bonds would do it.

• Tell your wife exactly where your life insurance policies are, and exactly where she should go with them in case you die (most likely the local agent of the companies issuing the policies). Life insurance may be the first cash from your estate to get into your wife's hands.

(Most of these suggestions until now have been based on the proposition that you are going to die. Well, you are, though not right now. Every study and statistic you can lay hands on will tell you that you will probably die before you wife does. It is in the years after you are gone that your wife will need your protection most, and you can provide a large measure of it by passing on to her now what information you have.)

• Tell your wife, in detail, just what income per month she can expect with you gone. You've already told her, maybe, what your pension will give her. Now tell her what her Social Security benefits will be (they'll probably change when you die), and just what your life insurance policies will do. Will they pay her, say, $40 a month for twenty years? Or for life? Will they pay her a cash settlement of, say, $10,000? Let your wife know if you would protect her.

• Show your wife your income tax returns of recent years, tell her why you filled them out as you did, and where they are kept. You probably made out your returns in the joint name of your wife, and you don't want Internal Revenue coming around to make claims when you aren't here. Explain to your wife, also, that she may have to make income tax returns herself if she is left, and as best you can, tell her how to proceed with the job.

• This is of particular importance. Tell your wife—then give her a letter confirming it which she can use as evidence—that you do not owe any debts she is not aware of, and that you have made no promises about money to anybody. Many widows these days are plagued by odd people showing up after the funeral to tell them you owed them this or that, or that you promised them something. Your letter will protect your wife from this racket.

• Tell your wife the person you want her to consult about her affairs if you should ever become unable mentally or physically to handle your affairs. It may be a lawyer, a minister, or a friend.

(Presumably, in passing all this information along to your wife, you also have passed her a ball-point pen and a sheet of paper. She'll not remember it all.)

• See that you have with the valuable family papers some photostatic copies of your birth certificate, marriage license, and military record. There'll come a time when your wife may need all of them. She is also going to need copies of your death certificate; she's going to have to prove to everybody, from Washington, D.C., to the county courthouse, that you really did die. Tell her where she can go to get a copy of a death certificate. And if you haven't done it yet, tell her where you've hidden the valuable family papers.

• Presumably any deeds, leases, and contracts you have are with the family papers. If not, tell your wife where you hid them.

• Finally, plan a serious evening session with your wife to talk about the handling of money, and try to determine how much she knows about it. Most husbands, down through the years, have refrained from teaching their wives anything about money. They still refrain, and as a result, the newspapers get some interesting stories about gray-haired widows buying uranium mines and running off with handsome sellers of oil wells. If there is any money in your name, or in your name jointly with your wife, see if your wife has any idea what to do with it if she ever has to make the decision alone.

Suppose, for example, you have $5,000 invested in the common stock of an American corporation. This seems a good deal here and now—to you. Would it be so two years after you died? Or could it be stock in a corporation that could go broke?

What you want to pin down in this talk with your wife is whether or not she would know how to watch the stock and how to get out of it if it began to turn sour. You should determine also whether she would know when to keep any savings in a local bank at 4 percent return, and when to send the savings to another state and get a 5 percent return. Or vice versa. Would your wife know not to speculate in, say, real estate? Would she have a yen to gamble? Would she be inclined, once your dominating hand is removed, to blow the money on a trip to the Costa Brava in the blind faith that Santa Claus would take care of her?

These questions you must answer in your more experienced and more sophisticated mind. If you decide your wife will be competent to manage what is left to her, then let her manage it without hobbles and forget the matter. But if you have doubts, then go talk to a lawyer, then to a trust officer at the bank, and explore the idea of setting up a trust fund of all you own, a trust fund that will be controlled by trustees and be concerned only with protecting the money and paying your wife a regular income out of it.

You don't want to make your wife *too* happy, of course—she might take up dancing, or something. So it's about time to wrap this subject up. But just in case you really are devoted to the lady and want to keep her smiling when you retire, you might paste up on the back of your bathroom door the following resolutions.

I resolve, as of the date of my retirement, that I shall:

Hang up my own clothes, put my shoes away, and put my dirty clothes in the laundry myself;

Not set out to steal the affections of my wife's dog;

Assure my wife at least two hours of freedom per day to do with as she pleases;

Assist in setting up a retirement budget for the household that gives my wife a set sum of Mad Money per month—the same sum I get;

Stay out of the kitchen except when I am specifically invited, or when specific agreed-on chores take me there;

Give my wife full authority to have her daytime friends visit her on any reasonable basis during the daytime hours;

Not use my electric razor while she is watching a favorite TV program;

Give myself not more than six months of rattling around the house before I find a personal interest to occupy part of my time and get me out of my wife's hair;

Wear shoes, except when in bed, and wear something over my undershirt when I'm in the living room;

Remember that it has been my wife who all these years has written the letters to our children, and kept them in touch with us . . . and refrain from attempting now suddenly to become the big shot with them.

Six

MAKING YOUR HUSBAND HAPPY IN RETIREMENT

It's going to be easier than you think to make your husband happy in retirement.

It'll take some effort and a lot of psychology, but after he has done for you all those fine things listed in Chapter 5, you'll be in high spirits.

The first thing you do is to insist that he have a good facial photograph made of himself on or near his retirement date. This is not for his vanity, and not for you to put on the piano, though he would probably like that. It's part of your technique of keeping him alive. This will make him very happy.

Let your husband do what he pleases with his copy of the photograph, but you quietly take one copy and place it among your private things. Put it in a chest or dresser drawer where you can get at it. Then plan to look at it every six months or so to compare it with how he looks at that time.

Somewhere along the line, men begin to break. The cheeks sag, the eyes seem to recess, the mouth grows flabby. A balding head and false teeth are not part of this—it's something else. It's a sort of deterioration. It can happen in the fifties. In some men in the eighties or later, but it happens. A wife who lives steadily with her husband can fail to notice the gradual process.

But if she has a photograph of him at sixty-five, she will know.

She will know what people who see him every year or so know, but wouldn't mention.

Knowing, she can take him to a doctor, look into matters relating to his rest, his diet, his nervous condition, and possibly do something to deter his growing old.

A happy husband, one would presume, is likely to live longer than an unhappy one. Since a husband is one of the most precious things an older woman can own, it behooves her to place his happiness, along with his photograph and ideas she can pick up in this book, on her wifely retirement program.

It is not intended to be cute, nor is it the mouthing of a man, to say that a husband is a precious possession for the retirement years of a wife. He actually *is* precious, and no amount of trading stamps will get you anything like him.

What Is a Husband?

A husband is protection. Not because he's a he-man any longer, but because he is a man and because he is present. Elements in society that might harm a woman living alone would not dare if there is a man in the house. Any sort of man.

A husband is reassurance. He can tell you that the awful storm raging outside won't blow the roof off, and explain why. He can tell you with authority that the noise you heard in the backyard was a cat.

A husband is a status symbol. By his very existence he makes you a wife instead of a widow. In business matters and in civic and social life there is more prestige in the former.

A husband is someone to talk to. This requires no elaboration, since you are a woman.

A husband is companionship. Loneliness remains one of the great crosses older people bear. Another human being, no matter what may be wrong with him, is a deeply satisfying thing to have around.

A husband is an invitation. The social customs of our time, though intended to be kind, have no mail today for the older extra woman. She fouls up the seating at a dinner party, is only half enough people for a couple at bridge, is a special responsibility for a hostess at almost any social function. But if she has a husband—that's different. American social life is based on "two of a different kind."

A husband is a manager. With more authority than any woman can muster he can fuss at the phone company, demand redress from a store for shoddy merchandise, and cut down to proper size the funny people one encounters who need some cutting. He also pays bills well—and fixes things.

A husband is an escort. He can take you down the avenue at night for a stroll, to a cocktail lounge, to a hotel for the weekend, and to all sorts of places a woman would be embarrassed to go alone.

A husband is a sweetie-pie. To some wives. Sometimes.

So, since your husband at retirement time is probably the only one you'll ever have, and since you may keep him longer if you keep him happy, the class on "Making Your Husband Happy in Retirement" will now come to order.

There is a sequence in the pattern of making a retired husband happy. This is because he goes through a series of changes from the time he puts his foot in the front door with his pension until . . . well, maybe two years later.

FIRST STAGE: TOLERATE HIM.   The husband who is freshly home in retirement has some of the characteristics of a two-year-old red-headed nephew who has come for a visit; some of the insecure seventeen-year-old; some of the proud college sophomore. Nearly all his characteristics are youngish, and at least at first are immature. Tolerate them. They will pass.

On the first workday after his retirement, probably a Monday, he will have made a big deal out of ignoring the alarm clock, with a good bit of conversation about how wonderful it is. He will then proceed to wake up at his usual time, tumble around in bed for a while trying to go back to sleep (because it is almost a matter of honor that he sleep late), then get up. Let him. Then give him about twenty minutes to rattle around the house. Then get up and follow him because he's getting bored by now, and he thinks he's hungry for breakfast.

Don't interrupt him at breakfast. He has a lot of things to say about how wonderful this is. About the poor devils who are just about now getting to work. About how he is going to have a splendid life in his retirement, and not foul it up as most men do. About the fine tributes paid him at the retirement party. About the really remarkable things he contributed to his employer during his career.

Agree with everything. And listen.

He won't be able to tarry too long at breakfast. He has some very important matters to take care of today. These matters will consist of a trip back to the job to get something he forgot. But while he's dressing there'll be a phone call. From the boss. Somebody can't find something. "They'll have a struggle for a while," he'll say as he goes back to his dressing.

As he takes off for the office he'll warn you to watch the phone for any calls that come in for him. He'll tell you he'll not be able to make it back home by lunch. Somebody at the office will want to take him to lunch, he thinks. Somebody won't. While the thing he forgot, whatever it was, will be handed to him by some employee on the run. And that will just about be that. He may run into a couple of fellows who are goofing around in a corridor. And they'll talk a bit, mostly about how fortunate "good old Charlie" is to be out of this mess. A boss, a colleague, or possibly a former subordinate may pass by—in a hurry, of course—to call out, "Happy landing, Charlie," or "You're a lucky stiff, Charlie," and go about his business.

"Charlie doesn't live here anymore"

This is your husband's first encounter with this fact of life. He doesn't quite understand it. He can't realize yet that the employer loves him still, that his old co-workers love him still, but that they don't get paid for passing the time of day with a retired employee.

90

He goes to lunch on his own. He has two beers instead of one. He feels deflated. But by the time he arrives home, at 3:30 or so, he'll present a fine front about the whole thing. Let him. He'll tell you how envious everybody was of him. Believe him. He'll say some of the fellows insisted on taking him to lunch. Believe him. And if his pocket change is three dollars short, just believe him when he says he spent this buying his old boss a couple of drinks.

Let him talk his way out of his dejection. Then, finally, tell him he had what sounded like an important phone call from a Mr. Jones at the office. Mr. Jones wanted him to call back.

He'll take care of that at once. Mr. Jones is a clerk in the personnel office at the company. He wants to tell your husband that he should notify the insurance company sending him his pension what his permanent address will be for the next twelve months. When your husband comes back to tell you a company executive wanted to discuss an angle of his pension with him, believe him. When he says, "I hope I'm not going to be bothered forever by the phone calls from the office—after all, I'm retired, you know," tell him you hope so, too.

The particular characterization given here may not be exactly the one that occurs in your house on the first day after retirement. But it's pretty close. And it's given not so much to let you know the specific things that will happen as to warn you that your husband will, on this day, think he is a celebrity of sorts, will want to act like an important man, and will be most pleased by any contributions you can make to his illusion.

Pet him along during the afternoon of this first day. Make a big fuss over anybody who may phone to congratulate him on his retirement. Serve him a good steak for dinner that night—oh, go on and do it. It won't bankrupt you.

On the second day of his retirement, when he turns on day-time TV and tells you he'll never sink low enough in retirement to watch that stuff, don't agree or disagree with him. Just keep quiet. He will be telling you that some of this daytime stuff is really not bad on about his sixth day.

On about the fifth day of his retirement, when he is getting no phone calls and is about to set out to plow up the backyard, tell him you've decided you don't want it done just yet. Maybe in about a month. And if he starts to remove the sixty-foot dead tree at the side of the house, talk him out of it. He has been an indoor plant too long to plunge into any tough physical projects at home. He must work up to them gradually. So use what wiles are necessary to restrain him to more moderate endeavors.

If he wants to go play golf every day, let him. He'll tire of it in about a week. Even if he can find men to accompany him, which he can't. If he wants to go fishing every day, let him. He'll tire of this soon, too. And run out of companions. If he catches any fish, and brings them home . . . well, there are limits to a wife's duty in making him happy. Let him clean them.

These first three or four weeks of a man's retirement are jumbled and trying times for him. And for you. Your husband will make many false starts at things he wants to do. He thinks. He will want to go into town a couple of times, probably, to talk to somebody who had mentioned earlier something about a possible job. Don't build up any hopes about this. There might be a job of sorts available, but likely below the status level and the pay level your husband would expect. If he should go out seriously to apply for a job, as a sixty-five-year-old retired man, he will be sorely disappointed. Not just because he doesn't find a job but because he discovers a retired man doesn't interest anybody. Unless there are very important reasons why he should have another job, discourage him from seeking one, if you can.

In these first three or four weeks, it would be wise for you to arrange as many extra activities for your husband as you can. Picnics, maybe. For the two of you. Short trips out in the country. Any kind of social affairs you can manage. Anything that will get him out of the house and occupy his mind. Anything that will begin to turn his thoughts from the company and his job.

It is a very rugged ordeal for a man who has worked on a schedule for forty years to be suddenly free and undisciplined. It is not funny, as some believe. It is almost a stripping of the gears in his mental and emotional machine. So he tries this, or that. He changes his mind. He grows fretful. He slips into moody periods. He struggles to adjust because he knows he must, but also because this is supposed to be so wonderful, this freedom of retirement. He wonders if maybe he's a freak or something. But he doesn't tell his wife he is struggling. Nobody else is around to tell. He goes it alone, as a rule, and in silence.

A loving wife must prepare for this episode of her man's retirement, and ride it out with all the tender loving care she can muster. She may have prepared earlier to take a trip with her husband as soon as he retired. As she watches him in these first few weeks, she may think a trip is the only solution. A trip would help. But it is better if she can ride out his fever without the trip, because his fever will soon pass, and the trip will be much more significant in a later sequence of making him happy.

(Tucked in here, where nobody will see it, is probably the best place to put sex. There may be some of it, what with the man being home all day, naps, and such. A wife might keep in mind that the hotter one makes a fire, the quicker it burns out, and govern herself accordingly.)

SECOND STAGE: WEAN HIM. As the fever of a husband's adjustment to his freedom begins to subside, his wife should devote serious thought to the more serious problem of cutting the umbilical cord linking him to his company and his career. He has to get on with a new life now. He had just as well get his mind off the old.

The husband who has held an executive job is usually the most difficult to wean. He has become used to precedence and special rights. He has glowed in the respect and compliments paid him by underlings. He has walked in pride as a member of the Speakers' Table Set.

These trappings of his job have been his vitamins. He will miss them mightily. Far more, in most cases, than he will miss the actual work he has given up.

A wife can't supply these trappings, any more than she can provide the excitements of his job. All of it went over the dam with retirement. So she must look for things that will substitute. And they don't include butterfly-catching.

93

In most marriages the wife can be the deciding force in maneuvering her husband into the new kind of life he must have. He is inclined to sit and think, to dwell more and more on the past. He will often keep at it until age eighty unless his wife prods him out of it. Gently, of course.

She cannot content herself, as many wives do, with being sweet and kind. Not if she expects retirement to be anything but a drag on her husband and herself. She must work, and maneuver, and direct.

It is in this stage, five or six weeks after retirement, that a major trip, or travel of any kind, can be most effective. The trip should be a long one, if possible. It should be a new trip—that is, it should show the husband things he has not seen before and provide experiences he has not had before. A four-week trip to Daytona, Florida, where he has gone for the last eight vacations to fish, wouldn't be it.

Returning from a trip that had been new enough to force different thoughts into his head, and long enough to tire him, a husband would normally be pointed in the direction of his new life. The home, the scene of his fever, the chairs where he sat and moped, the corners where he rattled around, would now appear less a snake pit and more a base of operations.

At this point, a wife can finally get down to cases with her man. He must do something with his life; he can't just sit it out. So what does he think he wants to do? It need be only one major thing, provided it absorbs him. But at least one major thing it must be. So, what?

You don't have to nag. But you may have to be persistent until, finally, he decides something. And, as stated, butterfly-catching isn't it. Such an activity just doesn't have the substance to satisfy a man who has been out in the forest killing bears for forty years. Hobbies of any kind usually don't have the substance. A husband can tear into a workbench, where he has a good array of tools, but there's a limit to how many bookcases he can make. Or shelves. Or flower boxes. He runs out of things to make, and he gets bored.

One wife, a Mrs. John F. Whitcombe, rode out the fever period of her husband's retirement well enough but ran into what she called a "stubborn mule" when she tried to make him get out of the living room and do something.

"We had moved to the suburbs two years before my husband retired," she said, "and had a nice little brick house. There wasn't too much my husband could do with it; so after his first rush of enthusiasm on make-work projects soon after he retired, he drifted into the house and sat.

"I didn't really mind . . . I like the fellow. But this was such an awful waste of a good man. And he couldn't be happy this way. He was going to waste away and die before either of us got around to enjoying retirement."

The Whitcombes had moved into a middle-class suburb that was predominantly occupied by younger married couples with small children. Such couples don't have much money to spend. Almost none had been able yet to acquire the tools and equipment which the Whitcombes had accumulated over the years.

"I decided," said Mrs. Whitcombe, "that we had a ready-made business for my husband at our back door—renting out to our neighbors, at a small fee, our power lawnmower, our automatic dryer, our vacuum, power tools, wheelbarrow, sewing machine, and anything else we had that the neighbors needed.

"My husband balked at the idea, naturally. He didn't want to get involved in that sort of business. He didn't want to charge neighbors for borrowing things. But I explained to him they didn't borrow; they pushed their manual mowers, wrapped their washed clothes over a line in the backyard, just didn't make things to sew. They would be embarrassed to borrow so often. But if they could use what we had for a small fee . . ."

The Whitcombes argued back and forth for a few weeks. Then Mr. Whitcombe finally, and with some misgivings, set up in one side of his two-car garage what he called The Rent Shop. He put there the movable things such as power mower and hand tools that renters could take back to their homes, and then he installed his wife's dryer, his larger power tools, and other things that renters would have to come use on the premises. The sewing machine went to the basement. He paid six dollars to have small

95

notices printed, announcing he was in business. He paid two neighborhood boys one dollar each to distribute them within a mile of his home.

The notices said that the idea of the business was not so much to make money, so all rental fees would be quite low. The idea was to be of service to neighbors—"after all, why should everybody on a street pay ninety dollars for a power mower when nobody uses it more than two hours a week and for only half a year?" The idea was also "to give a lazy old retired man something to do . . . but not too much."

It took only a few weeks for the The Rent Shop to catch on. And it became, as Mrs. Whitcombe had anticipated, a community center. Neighbors gathered to talk, to return something or get something, and debate their respective home projects. Young housewives brought their wet laundry over in red wagons to wait in line to use the gas dryer, or to gather in the basement where somebody was usually at work on the sewing machine.

"It seemed that we had neighbors around us all the time," said Mrs. Whitcombe. "We had never been so popular, and I think had never had more continuing pleasure."

"My husband became intrigued with the economics of his venture, and had a delightful time figuring out just how much per hour to charge for the use of our dryer in order to pay operating costs and build up a fund for a replacement.

"In two years he has upgraded almost everything we have by trading in old things for new. And there is no question he has been of great service to the neighbors. But these are beside the point—I wanted to make my husband do something that would make him happy and keep him breathing. I've done it."

To maneuver a husband into operating a thing like The Rent Shop in his garage—whether he has been an executive or hired help—is a bit on the bizarre side. But it often has to be. Because the more conventional pursuits aren't open to retired husbands.

You, as a wife, may have to draw on your best imagination to concoct an activity that will wean your husband away from thoughts of his job and his past glories. Don't be afraid to be bizarre. Don't think too much about what friends will say. You have the vital job of making a husband happy, and anything that will wean him away from his career will contribute to that.

The husband whose job was at the nonexecutive level is usually easier to wean than the executive. He doesn't have memories of the speakers' table bugging him. He doesn't have former colleagues in stiff white collars who are watching.

Whatever station in business or the professions your husband has occupied, the following may give some ideas of the type of activity that will wean him, and over the long pull make him happy:

- Pottery classes are about as low in the echelon of retirement activities as your husband can get. *However*, if you can send your husband to a pottery class with the understanding that he is going to study all the books he can get on the subject, then make pottery and open a jug shop on Main Street, you'll have something. Something to make and sell, something a profit can be made on—these are things a man who has worked for a living can get his teeth into.

- Hobbies—the whole lot of them from model trains to photography—are seldom good *unless* your husband is directed into an avenue on a hobby that will produce a salable product and make some money.

- A postretirement job does, on occasion, work out. But rarely. Your husband can crack his spirit over the turndowns of seeking a job, can grow stale and bored with the kind of job usually available to a man over sixty-five. Talk him out of seeking a job unless there is a good prospect that he can get a position as a consultant, or advisor, or some such, with the privilege of setting his own hours and with pay that is low enough not to jeopardize his Social Security, or high enough to make it worth his while to go through the red tape to get his Social Security back once he drops it.

- A small private business is generally the finest retirement activity for a husband. Explore with your husband the idea of starting a dog kennel on a small scale so as not to cut deeply into savings; of opening a secondhand furniture store, with an eye out for discovering antiques; of getting an area distributor-ship for a newspaper and hiring neighborhood boys to do the work; of leasing a small pond or lake and setting up a fishing heaven; and what else is there in your community that can attract some people and turn a small profit?

• Welfare, charity and do-gooder activities run rampant in every community where people retire. Tell your husband—firmly, if you will—that if one of the organizations wants him to volunteer his services, he will do so but only on a level that utilizes the talents that have been manifest in his career. In brief, he will direct one of their fund-raising drives, but he will not stuff envelopes. Of course, if your husband wants some pals he can find them in the welfare organizations. A good percentage of the retired people in town are there—working for free because they could find nothing else to do—stuffing envelopes.

• Politics is the second most fascinating activity your husband can embrace to wean him away from his career. If he can guess right, and go on the campaign trail for some candidate who will win, he will make many new friends, have an exciting time of it, and after election get himself an interesting paying job. But if he guesses wrong you're going to have to hold his hand for a while.

• One fascinating activity your husband can embrace is genealogy. Get him started on a study of his family history and he will become as absorbed as a six-year-old with alphabet soup. You may wake up some morning to find he has gone off to study tombstones in Massachusetts, or is cheating the grocery budget to write letters to people from England to Oregon. But you'll have him happy. And wondering what it was about his old job that he once thought was so interesting.

This about takes care of that. And if it seems that you, the wife, have had to do all the work, then that's just the way things are. Your husband, much like your babies whom you tended long ago, is simply not going to wean himself. He'll sit in a living-room chair, watch daytime TV, and mope.

His happiness, and therefore yours, will very likely depend on your adding "and wean when he's sixty-five" to the "love, honor, and obey" that you uttered so innocently so long ago.

THIRD STAGE: HOUSEBREAK HIM. In large measure, the housebreaking of a husband lies in indoctrinating him in the daily chores that must be done to keep a house running. He will be happier if he has a role in these chores, and he will be more in tune with you. The indoctrinating can be crude and authoritative. Or it can be done with feminine finesse. Do it the finesse way. But above all, don't make your husband your flunky. Do as many menial jobs as you ask him to do.

Beyond the chores, there are but a few things the retired husband must be taught. Show him, for instance, how two people can make a bed not in half the time but in a fourth the time it takes one person to make it. Nudge him gently to empty the daytime ashtrays. Tell him you don't mind if he watches daytime TV all day but that most of it is really for morons and since he is certainly not a moron you just hate to see him do it. Let him know he will really have to shave every day, though every other day he can do it lightly with an electric razor. Three nights a week—any three he chooses—he will have to wear a tie to dinner because he doesn't want to retrogress to a heathen, does he?

He will have to wear shoes in the house, except that about ten o'clock at night he can kick them off as he sits in the living room. He cannot go around in his undershirt. He must learn that the household will run on some reasonable schedule, with meals and housework coming at about the same time every day.

This housebreaking, oddly, will contribute to a man's happiness. He prefers to be civilized, but he will let down a lot of bars when he retires unless his woman, who has always been his civilizing force, restrains him.

FOURTH STAGE: RESOCIALIZE HIM. The social pattern the normal husband has set up for himself during his working years usually dies away when he retires. Much of the social activity both he and his wife have had has been involved with his fellow workers or with people with whom he had business connections.

These people as a rule will slowly switch their social affections from a retired man to his successor.

But even if they didn't, they would not be the best social life for a man who is retired. He might like to have a party on a Monday night—he can sleep on Tuesday; they want to wait for Saturday night. He might want to play golf at 9 a.m. on a Thursday; they can't. He might like to talk about pensions, fishing, and gardening; they want to talk about the company and business.

The husband frequently fails to understand the major social change that comes into his life with retirement. He is inclined, in fact, to feel resentment when he realizes old friends who still work are drifting away. It is your responsibility, as the wife, to explain away his resentments—it will make him happier—and to set about formulating a new social pattern for the two of you.

Many a retired husband, particularly if he thinks old business friends have dropped him, tends to go into a social decline that can lead almost to hibernation at home. There's no happiness in this. A wife, no matter how her husband protests, should accept invitations, send invitations, and in general promote any reasonable social contacts that will keep him in touch with other human beings.

A retired husband needs, in simple terms, two kinds of social friends:

• A few who will be his daytime playmates and a few who won't be dying next week.

You, the wife, can do much to provide both kinds. The daytime playmates will usually have to be other retired men. In your club work and your church work can you be on the lookout for other women who have retired husbands? Can you suggest to them that their husbands and your husband must have some common interests and could their husbands drop by for coffee next Tuesday and get acquainted with your husband? After all, they've got as big a husband problem as you've got. Maybe bigger.

After cataloguing the particular interests of your husband—

fishing, golf, roses, photography, whittling, or whatever—you might discreetly inquire about the particular interests of the ladies' husbands, and thus not waste your coffee.

About the only other daytime playmates for your husband will be men who work at night, who are usually too busy to play; and bankers, doctors, and executives, who are usually too rich.

As for some social friends who won't be dying next week, you will have to de-age whatever social activities you are accustomed to because you will have to cultivate some younger friends. Not thirty-year-olds, but some couples from forty-five to sixty or so. Which means you may have to cool off on your rook parties, dominoes, tea, and croquet, and stop showing stereoscopical slides in the parlor. You'll have to get with it, with gin-Scotch-bourbon. The lower you go in the age scale the more the gin-Scotch-bourbon, and something to eat.

It's not quite that bad. But nearly so. Make your home and your personalities gay and alive and you will attract the younger people to you. And these people will be coming to your funeral —you won't have to be going to theirs. Anyway, they're more fun.

FIFTH STAGE: REMARRY HIM.   Nobody has ever said much about remarrying the retired husband, but his retirement is something of a second wedding for both spouses. There aren't the overtones of a sofa and a stove on the installment plan, of pretty babies, of sex, of a mortgaged house, of everything colored wonderful. But there is the very real matter of a man and woman, dedicated to each other, who now come closely together for the first time since their vows. Without all the extraneous matter—the debts, the children, the striving, the job, the divergent interests.

It behooves the wife to make the most of it. For her happiness is no less than her husband's.

So rededicate yourself to this husband who has at last come home to live with you, to squeeze out of your closeness with him all the goodness that should be stored up in a union that has lasted so long. And, quite seriously, to solidify what is the only secure companionship a wife and her husband can get after sixty-five, which is the companionship of each other.

With the toleration, the weaning, the housebreaking, the re-socializing, now out of the way, remarry this man of yours, even if you do it secretly in your own mind. Maneuver your days so that you can be his steady companion, except for breaks you give him from the routine. Plan with him. Dream with him. Make your desires and discomforts his, and make his yours. Not to be a nice lady. Not to be good, or noble. But because it is in the close communion of a man and wife after sixty-five that the greatest happiness for both will lie.

Make no mistakes about this. If your husband is to get the deeper satisfactions of retirement, if he is to be happy, and if these can add to the years when he will be around to investigate the noises in the backyard and tell you how wonderful you are, his future lies in his togetherness with you.

And where, dear lady, if not in that same togetherness, does *your* future lie?

SEVEN

~

YOUR HEALTH IN RETIREMENT

Your health, as you move into retirement, won't worry you much. Unless you're losing it.

If you are like most people, you'll shudder a bit when you run into a cancer case, be sad for a day after you attend a funeral, and wrinkle your brow over what Medicare is all about (see next chapter). But you'll be inclined to brush aside any thoughts of your being ill or dying. That is, unless you've starting hurting somewhere.

This is not good enough. Nor is it good enough that you are a prompt payer on your health insurance policies.

Men and women can live a long time after their retirement date. They can live in reasonable comfort, and free of pain. Just how, nobody seems to know. But the best medical minds of the country have some pretty good ideas on the subject.

The best of them is to go see a doctor *now* before you have to. And let him see what makes you tick.

When a quite prominent businessman, who will be called Mr. Brown, retired from a good career in the East, he was vibrant and apparently was physically fit for a sixty-five-year-old man.

"I'm not about to turn into a turnip," he told friends at the company when he retired. "You'll be hearing about me."

103

Mr. Brown was confident of this. He would move into some new business venture, and he would take over an even more prominent role in civic affairs now that he had the freedom of thought and freedom of time to give his all to them.

Mr. Brown, who was an extrovert of sorts, moved quickly to exploit his business connections as soon as he retired. A position as a consultant was what he wanted, with a desk, secretarial help, and freedom to set his own hours. He got it. Men with business titles and good business contacts often can.

But Mr. Brown didn't hold it long. Most retired consultants don't. He was expensive to the company hiring him, and contrary to popular conception, he wasn't needed after five months. The company had a particular problem it thought he could solve. This is frequently the case. It also wanted to take advantage of the business contacts which the company didn't have but which Mr. Brown did. Once these two goals were accomplished, Mr. Brown was, politely, out.

This shook him up a bit. He spent about a week getting his confidence back, then moved to make another, similar connection. But now he was used merchandise. No company was particularly impressed by him, and he could find no job. He had overlooked the fact that a man retiring from a good career can sell himself as a retired man only once. After that the shine has worn off and he is secondhand.

Over a period of about four months Mr. Brown fought to make a second connection. He wasn't going to be a turnip. And the more rebuffs he got, the harder he tried, according to his wife, who takes up the story.

"I wasn't concerned that he was hurting his health through all this," she said. "I worried because he worried. I felt very bad when he came home in the afternoons with his fallen face. I had no reason to think he was harming himself."

Eventually, Mrs. Brown said, her husband decided he couldn't make the business connection. He then plunged almost viciously into civic affairs. "We didn't need the money from a job anyway. Our pension was good enough."

He renewed his memberships in all luncheon clubs and other

groups where he had been associated. He sought out other organizations to join. He volunteered to do charity work. He became an eager beaver in all the affairs at his church.

"At first, I thought this was going to be the answer for him. He was appointed to this and that, was telephoned all the time, had committee meetings, luncheons. He was the busiest boy you ever saw.

"But then something suddenly happened, just as it had on the consulting job. He began getting third-place and fourth-place positions in most of his endeavors. The chairmanships, the presidencies, the top offices, were going to young people, almost invariably to people who still had jobs. And because of their jobs had influence and importance my husband no longer had."

But Mr. Brown wasn't going to be a turnip. He went for the "fringe" welfare organizations, those that didn't matter much in the community. He even organized a semireligious group of his own. And where before he was giving five or six hours a day to his civic work, he would now spend up to ten hours in a day, striving to make his mark. He wasn't going to be a turnip.

"He had a stroke at one of his committee meetings," Mrs. Brown said. "He died before I could get to the hospital."

What killed him? Was it the striving and straining? Nobody knows. But certainly it would have been the better part of the gamble for the Browns to let their doctor look in on the husband's condition as he went through his rugged battle to retain his status. Could the doctor have advised something that would have avoided his stroke? You don't know. But he probably could have, and that probability is so vitally important that it's a little silly to pass it up.

Correct Your Ills

Any person coming up to retirement doesn't know the score if he or she fails to correct any physical problems while still a company employee and covered by the company health insurance.

A thorough health examination, by a doctor or a clinic, would be part of this. If anything is found that can be corrected, the time to correct it is before retirement. Even if it may mean loss of pay. There are three main reasons for this:

1. While a person is still employed, the company is The White Father, so to speak, and tends to look out for its people in a hospital, during an operation, or whatever.
2. The health insurance a person has while still employed is sometimes better than the Medicare a retired employee gets. In fact, all health insurance ends at retirement in some companies.
3. Retirement is a new beginning, a new life. Why start it with a stomachache?

The fact that you have taken care of this item of preretirement health planning is only the start. When retirement comes, you should establish contact with your own doctor and ask for a "consultation" appointment. Your husband or wife should go along to it.

There are specific things you should talk to the doctor about on this visit, and you might take this list along with you.

- Let him know what preretirement health steps you have taken.
- Outline your medical history, if he doesn't already have it.
- Explain to him the type of physical work you did on your job, and the exact type of activity you expect to engage in now.
- Ask him about sex, if you're still thinking about it.
- Discuss with him your retirement diet—such things as two meals versus three, sweets, fats, etc.
- Tell him any travels you plan and ask what health precautions you should take.
- Ask him how much sleep you need, how much exercise, and how many extra vitamins, if any.
- Tell him you'd like to live awhile, and therefore at what intervals should you come back for checkups and more consultations.
- Thank the man, tell him to send you a bill, and go home and do what he told you to do.

Now all this may not keep you on this earth for fifteen minutes longer than if you had never gone to see the doctor. But it very probably will. Anyway, in what might be called a matter of life and death, do you know any better bet than to trust him?

It would be helpful if the words written here could tell you whether or not you should play golf, mow the lawn, fuss at your wife or husband, sit, exercise, worry, get excited, or love cats. But no such words as these can because you are special, as every person is. Only a doctor who knows something about you can prescribe. And while he may not know all the answers, he knows a lot of them. And in the main he is a good and honorable fellow, is doing his best, and would much rather see you alive than dead.

You, being in the realm of age sixty-five, are a mustard-plaster kid. Castor oil, herbs, salves of all kinds, and patent medicines galore are your heritage. You grew up in an age when Grandma's remedies were among the best of medical science. A lot of this rubbed off on you and stayed. There is a lingering suspicion of a fellow in a white coat with a stethoscope around his neck. But this fellow is your best chance to stay alive.

It is important that you realize there is a large increase in yak-yak about health and ailments as people grow older. In this yak-yak you can get free information and advice about your physical well-being.

People will point out to you that you must take exercise after you retire, and call your attention to old Mr. Felix up the street who takes a long walk every morning and is now eighty-three. What is good for Mr. Felix may well kill you.

You will get all sorts of recommendations about taking vitamins, because somebody else is taking them. You will have patent medicines shoved at you. You'll not have a crony who doesn't know at least three remedies for the pain in the lower part of your back.

But you're special . . . remember? What helps fifteen other retired people can harm you.

Go on and see the doctor.

There's one grim fact about you and your health that you had just as well face up to now, then forget it. A sixty-five-year-old man or woman, as of today, is not living a great deal longer than people of sixty-five lived back in George Washington's day. A little, but not nearly as much as a lot of misinformation in recent years indicates. The statistics this country loves to play with are to blame.

The "span of life" over recent years has increased markedly, but the span of life they talk about usually includes babies. And babies never had it so good. Doctors have found many ways to bring them through the perils of infancy, which means a baby born today has a much better chance to reach age eighty than a baby did fifty years ago. It doesn't mean a sixty-five-year-old has.

To a nonmedical man who travels around among retired people there are indications that many of them are letting their minds turn them into semi-invalids. There are signs that medical doctors keep battling the puzzle as they strive to keep them well.

There is a fair chance that you will at least have a brush with the matter as you move into retirement. So you had better think about it for a minute.

Men, particularly, go into retirement with a monkey on their back. They are going to prove to everybody they'll not turn into a turnip. Or they find they can't adjust to leisure and grow morose. Or they grow frustrated with the nothingness retirement gives them and fly off on tangents. Or they watch old friends drifting away from them, think they are no longer worthy, and slip into mental depression.

In the throes of any or all these they make those around them miserable, are in turn avoided by them, and the vicious cycle grows worse.

Apparently one of the most common of the mind-inspired ailments is the retired person who pretends an illness to get attention. This happens to strong men and women who think they are above that sort of thing. It can start, for instance, on a morning when a newly retired man has a day of deadness coming up and just can't face it. (Don't laugh, because you, too, will have some days like this.) The man tells his wife he just doesn't feel like getting out of bed. Maybe it's a pain in the stomach. Maybe in the back. Or maybe something vague.

From this innocent beginning some men have never recovered, but have gone on from one mentally inspired ailment to another, always garnering the extra attention along the way, until tney turned into a vegetable and died.

It will be all right for you to hide under a sheet from a day you don't like, provided you do it only now and then and stay constantly aware that the trick is habit-forming.

Probably the second most common of the mind-inspired illnesses is fear of tomorrow. Most people who have worked for a living have a fixation about where money comes from: it comes from working. But they aren't working now. They aren't saying "sir" to anybody. They are getting money from Social Security and their pension, and everybody says these are sure and permanent, but they aren't working for this money. It's a new concept of things, this "free" money. And there are a good many retired people who begin to worry about it. Maybe the payments will stop. Suppose the pension company goes broke? What about a war?

Once a retired person starts worrying about this, he or she is off on a roller coaster. And there's no end to it short of the cemetery.

You might reflect for a moment on the fact that there are some serious complications, apart from physical illness, that can arise from any disturbed mental condition you allow yourself to fall into. The case of the Smith family, while not necessarily typical, is indeed possible. A friend of the family tells the story:

"Mr. Smith was the type who was prone to worry anyway. When he retired he had a field day. He was depressed by the usual things that depress a newly retired man. He took all his negative thoughts to his wife. He flew into tantrums when children and dogs came into his yard. He went downtown one day and came home drunk about 11 P.M. He began talking of taking the $7,000 savings he had to start a small business of his own.

"At this point Mrs. Smith, having gotten advice from friends, told her husband she wanted him to go see a psychiatrist.

"This was the equivalent of pouring gasoline on the fire. What did she think he was—a nut? And his condition grew worse.

"Mrs. Smith quietly persisted. And in due time Mr. Smith went under treatment by a psychiatrist.

"Nobody ever knew whether the treatments helped or not. Mr. Smith died of a cerebral stroke about six months later.

"He owned a farm, his house, and the $7,000 savings. He left no will. But he left an estranged son he hadn't seen in six years, and two maiden sisters who never liked his wife anyway.

"It was two years ago now that he died. The fight over his estate is still in the courts, and with the evidence of Mr. Smith's session with a psychiatrist flopping back and forth in the hearings the poor man is going to be established as incompetent, insane, senile, and probably plain crazy before anybody even gets a monument on his grave."

This couldn't happen to you. Of course not . . . Why the idea! Still, you'd better watch it.

Find peace of mind. In the church if that is the place for you. In reading the fine books. In going to a doctor if you think a doctor can help you find it. Or simply in being captain of your mind, and directing it into positive channels, toward the future, away from the yesterday of a job that won't be coming back, and from the facts of retirement life that you can't change.

Find peace of mind.

Where You Grow Ill

Probably the major health problem in retirement you must solve is the location where, if you must get ailments, you will get them.

The best of all places to grow ill, if you must, would be in your own home, in a community that had known you a long time, in a neighborhood where doctors make house calls, and near a drugstore with delivery service.

There is some comfort to an illness in familiar surroundings and in a home that has sheltered you for a long time. There are people who will come calling if the community knows you, and bring some petunias or a pie. And they will talk about you, sympathetically, and be genuinely concerned if your illness is serious.

An apartment would not have the warmth or the callers that your home would. It would less likely be on a house-call schedule for a doctor. In fact, people living in apartments who have long illnesses are the ones most likely to be transferred to a hospital, so the doctor can more conveniently make checks. Still, an apartment in your hometown is probably the second best place to grow ill, if you must.

A strange city—say, a dream town you had just moved to in retirement—would probably be the most miserable place for an illness. You wouldn't be too trustful of the doctor, because you wouldn't know him. You couldn't be sure you hadn't been shunted to a second-rate hospital and weren't being given second-rate attention because you were a newcomer. And worst of all, perhaps, you'd have nobody to talk to. Nobody to tell you the doctor was really all right, and so was the hospital. Nobody to be sympathetic. Nobody to send flowers. Nobody to phone your spouse to offer companionship or advice.

So, if you move to a new town when you retire, make up your mind you'll not become ill for at least two years.

Not long ago, an illness brought a double tragedy to one of those lush retirement resorts where the wealthy are wont to go, one of those golfing-cocktail settlements where you are sure you would be happy forever after if only you could afford to check in.

A couple had moved in about three years before at this resort and had become part of the social days that retired people concoct at such places. For a while everything was fine, then physical problems began moving in on the husband. A couple of days in bed at first, then a little later on a week in bed, then recovery for a few weeks followed by a month in a hospital—not an unusual pattern for one who begins to lose health in the seventies.

The hospital stay seemed to help for awhile. Then bed again, this time at home. Then a daytime nurse so the wife could have some freedom. Then a wheelchair. Then invalidism.

Sophisticated people who inhabit the fine retirement resorts do not probe in such cases. They perform the nice and proper acts, express sympathy, and go on about their business. Those dedicated to a social life, as many in these places are, are usually quick to go on.

This happened in the case of the wife with the invalid husband. In about three months, as a gay life swirled all around them, there were no more flowers, no more visits, no more expressions of concern. Just a nurse, a desolate wife, and a husband who by now had lost his hope.

Apparently by mutual consent—nobody ever knew for sure— the husband and wife decided one night there was no reason for going on, but that they wanted to stay together. The police found them dead the next morning.

So, if you've got $20,000 a year to retire on go ahead and try a retirement resort. But don't grow ill there.

There comes a time, even for the best of us, when infirmities creep up or when old or chronic ailments grow into daily problems. When such time comes, a reputable nursing home or a retirement home is the finest place you can be. Both types of homes come in many varieties. There are commercial homes, some of which are deplorable. There are homes sponsored by churches, by fraternal organizations, and by labor unions that are among the finest on earth.

Nursing homes, which in the main are concerned with older people, and retirement homes have one virtue as places to grow ill that you'll find nowhere else: their only mission in life is your health and well-being.

You aren't an embarrassment, a bother, an interference. You are the order of the day that the homes were set up for.

There are other places to grow ill—in the homes of children where you shouldn't live if you can avoid it but where you will get tender loving care if the children and their children can manage; in jail, where they say the bedside manner isn't so good; or in Arizona, where you can believe all they say about the curing powers of that sunshine and live in hope all the way to the grave.

Your Health and Money

Health costs money. Or, more accurately, the fight against illness and pain costs money. And the price seems to go up as you grow older.

But there is no set price for good health. You can't get a contract from anybody—not even a cost-plus contract—that specifies how much you will have to pay in six months or two years for what ails you. You may become a victim of arthritis and have to pay $5 a month for a visit to the doctor and $6 a month for pills for the next twelve years. Or you may become a victim of cancer and run up bills of $15,000 in the next eighteen months. There is just no way to know. So your best precaution, whatever medical benefits might be available to you under Medicare, is to buy from a private insurance firm some sort of "disaster" health insurance, something on the order of the "deductible" policy on automobiles. If, for instance, you see your way clear on medical bills that may run to $2,000, take out insurance for everything above that figure.

Many companies have such insurance. The fees are not high.

Oddly, the poorer you are in retirement, the better medical care you can frequently get. Just go to a welfare agency or a public hospital, declare your inability to pay, and go into a welfare hospital bed. The finest services of a community's finest doctors are given here without charge.

There are no "Hurt Now—Pay Later" plans set up for medical care. All along the line, except perhaps for the doctor, you will have to pay cash. So it would be advisable to have your eye on ways to get your hands on some money fairly quickly—just in case. You can borrow on, or cash in, any securities you have. You can get a mortgage on your house, or if you already have one can probably get additional money on it. You can usually get immediately any funds you have in a bank or savings and loan association. You can probably get a loan, or a cash payment, on any life insurance policies you have.

You would be doing your children a favor if, after you retire, you inform them of any major health problems you see coming up that you won't be able to pay for. In some cases your children could be forced to pay any medical costs you have. In almost any case they would feel such moral pressure to help you that they might wreck themselves financially to come to your aid. In recent years the children of many retired parents have volunteered to pay premiums for "disaster" health insurance for them just to avoid such crises.

You should be aware of these financial angles of your health problems, though most of them are negative. You should make mental notes of this and that, and look into the insurance idea. Beyond that there is little point in depressing yourself about the matter. After all, you could worry every day about it. At night, too. But it would be about the same as worrying over a tornado that might come down your street tomorrow.

Health Notes

Now for some health notes, more on the positive side than some of the information that has gone before.

• You probably aren't going to have a disastrous illness. Most people don't. So don't let yourself get preoccupied with the matter of your health. That's one of the best ways to grow ill—think long enough about your stomach, or talk enough about it, and it'll soon show up aching for sure. You will find as you associate with other retired people that many of them are obsessed with their physical being, and always they have ailments. Use a little common sense about this, then get on with your retirement.

• Take a good hard look at the health practices you have always followed, and particularly at such things as vitamins and patent medicines you have become addicted to. Ask your doctor if they are really necessary, or if they are actually just a mental crutch for you. More than a few people go into retirement saddled with a $10-a-month outlay for some sort of tonic or such they have taken for the last seven years because they are quite sure it makes them feel better. Well, maybe it does. Or maybe it's in the same class with the story of the man who took an ounce of whiskey every morning for five years because it made him feel better, he said. As a matter of fact, his system had become so conditioned to it in five years he would have felt drunker if he skipped it some morning. Just ask the doctor.

• You may be going into retirement without a regular doctor, or you may be moving to a new town. How do you choose a doctor? You can ask neighbors, or friends, who will recommend their own doctor. He may or may not be best for you. You can test by making visits to a list of doctors you get from the phone book. But this is expensive, takes time, and will probably get you so confused about yourself you won't know whether you're cracking up or not.

You can ask the man behind the prescription counter at the drugstore. You can close your eyes and guess.

One of the more intelligent ways to choose a doctor is to phone the office of the county medical association (nearly every county has one), or phone a nearby hospital. In each case you will be seeking a particular kind of doctor; a general practitioner is often best for retired people because he can recommend any specialist you might need. Both the association and the hospital will give you several names, but the hospital will likely give you names of doctors who are on its staff, which could be important to you if you ever need to go into that hospital.

Make your choice from the names you get, and unless there are potent reasons for changing, stick to the fellow you choose. He can become your friend over the retirement years, but more importantly if he can watch you over the years, he will be in a better position than anybody to cure what may come up to ail you.

• In choosing a drugstore for your medical supplies you don't have to worry much, provided you are in a reasonably well developed community. Many of the drugstores are chain units these days, and just about all of them maintain high standards. But, as mentioned earlier, you might see if the store has delivery service. Just in case you want a prescription refilled some afternoon when it's raining.

• If you have ever been in active military service, make sure you determine the location and practices of any Veterans Administration Hospital that is within reach of where you live. Your congressman, or possibly your post office, can tell you of any nearby establishments. The Veterans Administration is rather fond of former service people, and when they become ill it tries all sorts of ways to provide medical help for them. You may not be eligible for treatment in such a hospital. But you won't know until you try.

• After you check the tax rate and temperature charts of any new town where you are moving, if you move, have a look at the availability of a hospital and the supply of doctors. Some of the smaller towns where people go in retirement have neither doctors nor hospitals.

• Finally, get an examination of your eyes and your ears. This could be the greatest retirement gift you could hand yourself. It would cost a little money. The hearing of many people grows weaker by retirement time. This is all right with a lot of them because they know by then that about half the stuff they hear isn't worth it anyway. But there is danger in impaired hearing— shouts of warning, approaching cars, and cries for help go unheeded. The slight crackle of a fire in the basement at night, the soft steps of an intruder in the house, are too vital for any person to be unaware of.

But, primarily, the retired person who can't hear well will miss much of the pleasure of the later years because the audio of life is now all around, particularly in television and recording, both of which contribute greatly to retirement. Then there is the matter of conversation. Some of it is worth hearing.

You may have lost much of your ability to hear without realizing it; almost anybody at age 70 who can't hear a freight train will protest strongly that he or she hears as well as anybody. So have an examination and see. Don't be bashful about a hearing aid if you need one.

If you can't see very well you are likely to protest even more loudly than the half-deaf that your eyes are as good as anybody's. And you aren't pretending. You believe it. But a funny thing happens on the way to age sixty-five. Along in the mid-fifties you had your eyes checked and probably changed your glasses. In the early sixties you saw no need to check again because your days of working were about over, and you could see quite well enough. But somewhere along now you began cutting down on your reading. It made you sleepy. Or the things to read weren't as good as they used to be. Or something. With increasing frequency you laid newspapers and magazines aside and looked at television, or just sat.

Now, with retirement, you have about given up what probably could be your greatest treasure—the printed word. The accounts of what happened today, the works of the novelists and playwrights, the magnificent stories of mankind's struggle to the present, and even the Bible are beyond your reach if you can't see well enough to read them. Television, great as it is, can't touch the pleasure you can get from reading.

An eye examination and posssibly new glasses would let you read. Some 150-watt lamp bulbs beside your chair wouldn't hurt either.

It may be pertinent to tell you that many publishers of books and pamphlets for retired people now print such things in larger type, just like for the kiddies. Not because you're kiddies, but because the publishers know you have neglected your glasses and can't see too well.

POSTSCRIPT: There is much talk abroad in the land that the climate of one state is better for your health than another. You hear stories of doctors ordering retired patients to move to Arizona to get the sunshine, or flee from the rugged winters of the Midwest.

Well, there may be something to all this. And there may not.

117

In about every state in the United States for about four months of the year there is enough hot sunshine for an army of invalids. A retired person living in the Midwest snows can acquire a freezer, store up food, and remain in a cozy home for three weeks on end.

Before you rush off to the faraway for a climate that will help your health, figure out if you can get a lot of that climate right where you are, and then go ask your doctor what he honestly thinks.

EIGHT

MEDICARE AND MEDICAID

Medicare is what *you* will get when you reach sixty-five. Medicaid is what your poor relatives will get.

That's putting it broadly, but it pretty well denotes the significance of the two great medical programs that the federal government has brought to the people in recent years. Medicare has the American eagle stamped all over it and comes directly from Social Security to you. Medicaid as a rule comes through the states and counties, with the federal department of Health, Education, and Welfare supplying most of the money.

Medicare is essentially an insurance program, with the premiums assessed by the government. Medicaid is essentially a welfare program. But Medicaid is regarded by many experts as the sleeper of the federal health programs—the crowbar that will eventually pry open the door to socialized medicine for everybody. (More on this later.)

Medicare

This is the Santa Claus of people reaching age sixty-five since the mid-1960's. They have been getting one part of it free, and the other part for half a premium. By contrast they have been paying for their regular Social Security benefits for most of their working years.

The free part of Medicare is called Hospital Insurance—Part A. The half-premium is called Medical Insurance—Part B. On Part B you pay $5.60 a month and the federal government pays $5.60. (But watch this. The premium is based on what services cost, and may go up several dollars more in your lifetime.)

In general, all persons eligible for Social Security or railroad retirement benefits are eligible for Part A Medicare when they reach age sixty-five. So are wives of eligible workers when they reach age sixty-five, if they'll ever admit they're that old.

From this point on, as with your income tax return, things get a little complicated. For instance, it gets a bit tougher every year to cash in. If you became age sixty-five prior to 1968 you and everybody else could get Part A of Medicare whether or not you had credit for any work under Social Security. But in 1968 you needed three quarters of credit to get it, in 1969 six quarters of credit (or coverage), and in 1970 nine quarters. The schedule from 1970 on reads like this:

You reach age sixty-five in	Quarters Needed	
	Men	Women
1971	12	12
1972	15	15
1973	18	18
1974	21	20
1975	24	21

A quarter of credit is three calendar months in which you are paid fifty dollars or more in wages.

As stated, this is a general picture of what eligibility requirements are. But there are a lot of "whereas" clauses and a lot of footnotes in Medicare regulations. For instance, if you want to work beyond age sixty-five, you are still entitled to Part A at age sixty-five. On the other hand some federal employees who are not eligible for Social Security or railroad retirement benefits can't get Part A, but can sign up for Part B. That sort of thing.

So if your name is not John Smith and you didn't work for a straight $100 a week for thirty straight years under Social Security, go ask the pretty girl behind the desk at the Social Security office just where you stand. And make sure you go at least three months before you reach age sixty-five.

Bear in mind also that Medicare is growing and changing almost every time the Social Security officials come back from lunch. Even if you are a "standard" case, the regulations covering you may have changed since last week. So just go ask the pretty girl behind the desk.

Remember now, Medicare is in two parts—Part A and Part B. This is still Part A we're talking about, and as of the most recent check Part A brings you three types of benefits:

As a bed patient in a hospital;
As a bed patient in an extended care facility;
As a patient at home.

As a bed patient in a hospital. You will get under Part A, if your doctor okays you, about all the services you would normally get as a paying patient in a hospital, but no private room or television set. You will get:

A bed in a semiprivate room (two to four beds)
All meals, including special diets
Operating room charges
Regular hospital nursing services
Drugs furnished by the hospital
Laboratory tests
X-ray and other radiology services
Medical supplies such as splints or casts
Use of wheelchairs, crutches, braces, etc.

You get all this for free for sixty days, except that there's a $68 catch in it. You must pay the first $68 of the total hospital bill, which Social Security says is to help defray the costs of the program but which is really a device to discourage the neurotics.

Now after you've been in the hospital for sixty days for free

121

(minus the $68) you get another thirty days under **Part A**. But for these thirty days Medicare makes you pay $17 a day of the costs. In addition to the extra thirty days you get a "Lifetime Reserve" of sixty additional days which you can call on at any time you need them. Part A pays all costs here except for $34 a day.

Again things get complicated . . .

You get your sixty days of free hospitalization, and your thirty days of $17-a-day hospitalization, for each spell of illness or for each "benefit period," as Social Security prefers to call it. You get as many benefit periods as you want *provided* you let sixty days elapse between them.

In very simple language this means you should be sick enough to stay in a hospital for only sixty free days, then refuse to be that sick for the next sixty days. Nobody has figured out yet just how to schedule hurting this way, but that's the trick if you can manage it.

There are special rules covering the benefits you get in a psychiatric hospital. But see if you can go to an infants hospital instead. The country has been on a "mental health" kick for some time now, and if it keeps on much longer we're all going to be classified as nuts. But especially the older people. Heirs wanting to get their hands on an older person's money, spouses who are weary of the union but can't get a divorce, and even neighbors whose dogs are spoiling a cranky old man's petunia patch—all these are potential allies to the "mental health" promoters. And would be quite pleased to get you snatched into a psychiatric hospital where you might never get out and where there would be evidence to support legal suits to declare you mentally incompetent to handle your money.

So go to an infants hospital, a tuberculosis sanatorium, or anywhere except a psychiatric hospital if you can arrange it.

As a bed patient in an extended care facility, where you might go after leaving the hospital, you would get under Part A about what you'd expect from a good nursing home. At this time, presumably, you would not need the special care hospitals offer but would need skilled nursing care and other health facilities you can't get at home.

In this extended care facility Part A would pick up the tab for the first twenty days in each benefit period, this benefit period being the same one you had for your hospital stay. That is, if you were in the hospital only forty days of your free sixty-day benefit period, then you could pick up the next twenty days in the extended care facility. You could have an additional eighty days in an extended care facility, but you would have to pay $8.50 a day for this.

Now you can't just walk into an extended care facility and tell them to nurse you. You get the service only if:

• A doctor determines that you need extended care and orders such care;

• You have been a qualified patient in a hospital for at least three days in a row before your admission;

• You are admitted within fourteen days after you leave the hospital;

• You are admitted for further treatment of the condition for which you were treated in the hospital.

In the extended care facility you get the same general type of service you got in the hospital:

> Bed in a semiprivate room
> All meals, including special diets
> Regular nursing care
> Drugs furnished by the facility
> Physical, occupational, and speech therapy
> Splints, casts, etc.
> Wheelchairs, crutches, braces, etc.

You don't get color television. Or free delivery of *The Wall Street Journal*. Or pretty girls to hold your hand.

As a patient at home, Part A of Medicare will come visiting. It will come visiting one hundred times in a year after your discharge from a hospital or extended care facility. But only if:

• You were a qualified hospital patient for three days in a row;

• You are confined to your home;

• A doctor decides you need home health care and sets up a home health plan for you within fourteen days after your discharge from a hospital or extended care facility;

● The home health care is for further treatment of a condition for which you received services as a bed patient in a hospital or extended care facility.

Under the home health benefits you get part-time nursing care from a recognized home health agency; physical, occupational, and speech therapy; part-time service of home health personnel; medical social services; medical supplies by the home health agency. No drugs. No meals.

Intermission

A general picture of what Part A of Medicare is has now been given. Before you get into Part B you had better have a cup of coffee and muse over a few facts of life.

As you will note from Part A, the doctor is given a position at the right hand of God in determining what health needs you have. He's a better man to have this power than, say, the man who cleans the rest rooms. But for Social Security—or you—to ascribe to doctors any nobility other mortal men don't have is naïve. Doctors breathe, strive, love money, and go to the bathroom just as everybody else does. So keep this in mind as you join the Medicare set.

Have a doctor who's a good guy. One who knows you and likes you, and knows you pay your bills. He's much more likely than a stranger to find that you need to be sent to a hospital, that you need care in an extended care facility, that you need home health care. Human nature, you know—you've heard about that.

Make sure that this doctor, who is a good guy, has the patience and the secretarial help to handle all the annoying forms he'll have to fill out for Medicare.

Make sure that this doctor has the clout to get you into a hospital when you need to go. Some doctors, outside the hospital set, can't. Maybe they can in a week or two. If possible, determine whether this doctor will remain your doctor once you go into the hospital. In some towns local doctors can't treat their patients in a hospital; they have to assign them to a specialist on the hospital staff, then stay out of the way.

In general, most hospitals have now qualified themselves to handle Medicare patients. But not all of them. So don't move away to some hick town where Medicare doesn't work. And where the doctors have enough neurotic and rich old ladies on their appointment calendar to tell you to get lost. Intermission over.

Part B of Medicare is what is known as Medical Insurance. In essence, it pays the doctor. Social Security likes to stress the point that Part B is voluntary. So, too, is Part A, since you are entitled to it automatically when you reach age sixty-five. But Part B costs you. If you don't want it you don't take it.

But you should take five minutes of thinking before you turn it down. It's a good deal, what with Uncle Sam also paying half the premium and what with doctors' yen to charge more and more every time a Medicare patient shows up.

Part B, with certain limitations, will pay for:

Medical and surgical services by a doctor of medicine or osteopathy;

Services by podiatrists which they are legally authorized to perform by the state;

Services which are ordinarily furnished in the doctor's office, such as diagnostic tests, medical supplies, and drugs and biologicals which can't be self-administered.

Things Part B doesn't cover include:

Routine physical checkups;

Dental services, except for surgery of the jaw or related structures or setting of fractures of the jaw or facial bones. No cleaning, fillings, or pulling;

Routine foot care;

Eye examinations for prescribing eyeglasses, or ear examinations for prescribing hearing aids.

There are a good many borderline cases of what you can and

can't get under Part B insurance. The doctor or the hospital has experts around who can tell you.

Whatever services you do get under Part B, you get them anywhere the doctor treats you—in his office, the hospital, extended care facility, your home, or in a group practice clinic.

Now, as stated earlier, there are limitations to what you can collect under Part B. You must pay the first $50 of your doctor bills in any calendar year, January to December. You also can collect only 80 percent of the bills from then on. For instance, you become ill in February and before you're well again in July the doctor has billed you for $500. You pay the first $50, leaving $450. Part B pays 80 percent of this, or $360, and you pay 20 percent, or $90. Thus, a $500 doctor's bill has cost you $140 total.

Again, there are many exceptions in Medicare rules—in Part A as well as Part B. But the information given here applies to most people. If you think you have an exceptional case, your doctor or the hospital can tell you what you get.

Under Part B you get certain benefits as an outpatient. You're an outpatient when you go to a hospital for treatment but do not become a bed patient. With the same formula of $50 deductible and 20 percent of the remainder of the bill, you get laboratory services, X-rays, emergency room services, medical supplies, such as casts and splints. No routine checkups, no eye or ear examinations when given to provide glasses or hearing aids, no immunizations unless directly related to another ailment.

Part B also provides coverage of physical therapy services when furnished under the direct supervision of a doctor. The services can be given by a hospital, extended care facility, home health agency or public health agency, or a clinic.

In an extended care facility, or even in a hospital when you have exhausted your benefits, Part B (under the usual formula) will help you pay for:

Diagnostic tests
Radiation therapy
Surgical dressings, casts, etc.
Certain ambulance services

But Part B will not help you pay for any prescription drugs or drugs you can administer yourself. No hearing aids, eyeglasses, false teeth, or orthopedic shoes.

You get about the same home health benefits under Part B as you do under Part A (Hospital Insurance) *except that* Part B doesn't require that you be hospitalized before you get them. Also, in certain cases Part B benefits are in addition to what you get from Part A; for instance you get one hundred home health visits a year in addition to the one hundred you get under Part A.

In general Part B supplies in the home (under the $50–20 percent formula):

> Part-time nursing care;
> Physical, occupational, or speech therapy;
> Portable diagnostic X-ray services;
> Rental or purchase of medical equipment prescribed by the doctor, such as a wheelchair or oxygen tent;
> Medical supplies furnished by the home health agency that has your case;
> Medical social services.

There are no drugs or biologicals, no personal convenience items, no meals.

On both Part B and Part A of Medicare, the Social Security people seem to make a special point of the methods by which the insurance is paid. Things aren't quite that complicated. When you get benefits under Part A at a hospital, extended care facility, or at home, the institution or agency involved makes the claim directly. You don't have to bother. Your grief comes when the institution or agency bills you directly for any services Medicare doesn't cover.

On Part B the doctor makes application directly to Medicare for his bill, or he can bill you and let you get the insurance yourself. If he bills Medicare directly, his fees must be what Medicare calls "reasonable." Some doctors don't like this, so they bill you and let you fight it out with Medicare. But they will hold you to their bill, no matter what Medicare agrees to pay.

Medicare has the doctors in something of a bind on this. If the doctor goes along with what is "reasonable" and bills Medicare, he is sure of collecting, since Medicare has plenty of money. If he prefers to bill you, he many never get all his money simply because you may never have that much. He's also in a bind on ethical grounds: if Medicare says his charges aren't reasonable, why should you be a patsy and keep patronizing him?

There are forms in all of this, some of which you have to fill out yourself. But don't worry about it. Anybody you owe money to will most likely have plenty of forms around, with somebody to show you how to fill them out quickly.

One final thing about Medicare. When you apply for it you get a pretty little card that shows your special Medicare number, name, etc., and whether you're qualified for Part A, Part B, or both. It'll fit neatly in your billfold if you'll throw away some of those silly credit cards.

Medicaid

The official name of Medicaid is Medical Assistance. It has special provisions for persons over age sixty-five, but applies in the main to everybody in need of medical services they can't afford. And it seeks to provide just about everything they need.

Medicaid is a part of the Social Security Act, and its regulations provide free medical services to families with dependent children; to the aged, blind, and permanently disabled whose income and resources are insufficient to meet the costs of necessary medical services; to those needing rehabilitation and other services to attain or retain independence or self-care.

These regulations are so broad, depending on the motivations for generosity on the part of those administering the program, that Medicaid has been interpreted as being possibly everything medically to everybody. Which is why it is regarded as the foot in the door of socialized medicine.

Medicaid is essentially welfare. Where Medicare, both Parts A and B, is insurance, with premiums paid by past, present, and future recipients, Medicaid is free. It is provided by grants from federal, state, and sometimes county governments.

All states don't offer Medicaid. Those that do don't all offer the same benefits. To get Medicaid, a state must come up with a program meeting minimum standards set by Social Security, then apply for a Social Security grant. This is normally the majority of the overall cost. The states provide the remainder of the money, sometimes dividing the costs with the counties.

States in the East and in the West have been in the forefront of the Medicaid program.

Medicaid can give you all that Medicare does, plus drugs, eyeglasses, and dental care and a vast array of services to cure whatever ails you and get you back on your feet once the ailment is cured.

Medicaid is welfare, but welfare doesn't have the stigma it once had. All sorts of nice people seem to be getting it these days. So if you, as a retired person, think you need it (and one state has recently said that if medical costs would reduce a person's money left for food, clothing, and shelter, he needs it), then shelve your pride and apply for it.

Just where to apply might give you some problems. But be persistent and some nice woman will eventually sit you down at her desk and start asking you questions.

In some states the whole Medicaid program would be administered by the state or county welfare department. In others the program would be fragmented, part of it going to the state board of health, some to the office handling aid to dependent children, some to the welfare department, some to whatever agency there might be to help the blind.

Your best first step would be to ask your local office of the welfare department (see the phone book) or the local Red Cross office (see the phone book) or your representative in the state legislature (somebody at the courthouse can tell you his name).

So far as can be determined you will get from Medicaid the same quality of medical services you would get from Medicare or from private hospital insurance, or from your bank account, because all along the line people who give you the services are being paid—much too handsomely, some say. So don't worry about this.

In an age when government at all levels is striving to give to all people what they say they need, don't hesitate to ask for Medicaid if you think you need it.

~

NINE

YOUR LEGAL AFFAIRS IN RETIREMENT

A man by the name of Wilbur K. Stephens reached retirement without ever once consulting a lawyer. About a year later income tax authorities challenged deductions he had made over the last two years on his returns, a challenge that could clobber his retirement savings. He went to a lawyer. He won the case. As a result, he asked the lawyer to start preparing his income tax returns for him, and for the last three years has been saving around $100 a year on the returns, after payment of $50 per return to the lawyer.

A career woman, who will be nameless, became engaged to a sixty-six-year-old widower. She was fifty-six. Friends advised her to talk to a lawyer about making some type of written financial arrangement with the man before the marriage. She scorned the idea. She resigned from her job and married. Two years later her husband died. She was left alone, without a job, with $1,000, and with two years to go before she could get Social Security. Her husband had quietly passed all he owned on to the children of his first wife.

A certain Mr. Eugene Connors sold his home when he retired and moved South. He had his lawyer draw up all papers on the sale. Four months later he was sued for $2,500 by the buyer of the house because failure of pipes under the house caused collapse of the plumbing system. Mr. Connors referred the matter to his lawyer, who pointed out to the buyer that the sales agreement, as signed by all parties, held the seller blameless for such a default. That was the end of that.

And there was another instance, involving a Mr. Smith. He rebuffed all pleas that he make a will, then died without one. Under the laws of his state, in such a case, one third of what he owned went to his widow and two thirds went to his children. He owned a valuable farm, a house in town, and $22,000 in stocks. Fours years after his death his five children (abetted by their spouses) were still locked in bitter conflict over how to get their hands on one fifth of a two-thirds interest in a farm, house, and $22,000, while the poor widow longed to be out of the whole mess.

These four cases point up the vital role that lawyers—whether you like them or not—may play in your retirement. You should give some serious thought to this whole question because, whether you like it or not, you cannot go safely into retirement without some sort of legal assistance.

This is no advertisement for lawyers. It is simply the fact that when you come up to retirement the very things that confront you make it more necessary than ever before in your life that you obtain a lawyer's help.

Wills, or the lack of same, are governed by state laws, and there are now fifty states. Which means there are fifty different ways to die and leave your assets to your heirs. In general you do this in one of two ways: with a will, or without one.

Without a will, the state takes over distribution of the estate, and some state laws specify that half of all you own belongs automatically to your wife, plus a fraction of the half that belongs to you. Other state laws specify—if you have no will—that one third of what you own goes to your wife and two thirds go to your children. There are others. Public authorities, with the assistance of lawyers, would handle matters in most cases.

Court costs, lawyer fees, etc., can be as much, or more, when an estate is distributed without a will. The lapse of time before heirs get their hands on the money can be as much, or more, without a will.

The primary reason you should have a will is that it allows you, in your gray-haired wisdom, to decide who shall get the estate you have built up during a lifetime. Which is quite a nice decision to have. Most state laws won't allow you complete freedom in this, such as leaving your wife penniless while enriching a girl friend at a nearby saloon. But you have wide latitude, and a lawyer is the only one who knows just how wide.

A secondary reason for a will, which some men would consider the primary one, is that it tends to build a wall of fortifications around your estate. An estate that is protected by a will can be challenged in court, and often is. But a will that has been properly drawn, as a lawyer can do it, is tough to crack.

On the other hand, an estate that is not protected by a will is vulnerable to all sorts of attacks. You, as a man, may or may not have had an affair with a woman in the next county and a baby to show for it. But if that woman sues for part of your estate to support the child, your estate will be far safer if a comprehensive will has been left behind.

This wall of fortifications a will builds for you can also protect your estate from family squabbles that can tear your loved ones apart once you are in the cemetery. Some of the saddest of family tragedies come from the failure of parents to make wills that set out specifically what the surviving spouse and the children will get. Even such items as a grandfather's clock in the living room or linens that have the family initial can make brothers and sisters stop speaking to each other for forty years if there is room for dispute over who gets them.

Where money or property is involved the emotions of heirs can flare even more, of course, and in almost any civil court docket you can find case after case of family members suing each other because a departed parent did not leave behind a legal document—normally a will—stating precisely who would get what after the funeral.

There's another small angle here for you to ponder. Presumably you love your wife. With your children now grown your greatest concern would be for her security in case something happens to you. But you make no will. You die leaving your wife behind. And you are in a state where, without a will, only one third of all you own goes to your wife. Can your wife exist on one third of what you've got?

Your children, naturally, would take care of *your* wife, *their* mother. *Your* children would never start a family squabble over what you left. Would never even dream of suing one another.

Well, maybe. But all across this land children whose parents thought they were as noble as you think your children are do about every dastardly thing in the book if it's a matter of money. You see, your own children, even if good and true, aren't always the masters of their actions. By the time you die they are married, and their spouses, for good or evil, are exercising more influence on them than you or anybody else. Few children, including yours, would ever go out coldly and break up their family over money you left or neglect the needs of their mother because you didn't leave her enough. But spouses are a different pan of fish. Even a good daughter-in-law can prod her Horace to plunge in and fight for "what's his" if you left your money in a position where it can be fought for.

The manner in which you write your will must depend on your particular family obligations and your loves and prejudices. One method which has now gained wide acceptance is for the husband and wife to go to a lawyer together and each write separate wills. Usually they specify that everything each has will go to the survivor, and when the survivor dies the children or other heirs will inherit what remains. The husband and wife agree at this point just how each heir will benefit, and thus both wills read the same on this score.

There are husbands—maybe you included—who have kept all family assets, from the house title to the bank accounts, in their own names. They choose to be the hero, the sole dispenser of loot to their heirs, and thus eliminate their wives from will-making. They specify, first, protection for their wife, if they are good men, and then specify that when she dies Johnnie will get this, Mary will get that, and Susie will get so-and-so. This makes Daddy a fine fellow and Mama an also-ran. It's a sad reward for a wife who over the last forty years has helped her husband build what he will leave. It is frequently a serious detriment to the happiness and help a widow can get from her children. Because if Daddy's will specifies they will get certain benefits, they very probably are going to get them just that way. They don't have to be beholden to Mama. And sometimes they will tell her so.

On the other hand, if a husband leaves all he has to his wife (or vice versa) and allows the survivor to determine how each heir will benefit, it gives the survivor a strong hand in dealings with the heirs—and also some magic charm.

There are husbands—maybe you included—who have reason to doubt the financial judgment of their wives, and thus draw wills that keep all assets out of the wife's hands but provide her all income from them. In such cases it is gracious for the husband to say in his will that *"Mother* and I have decided" just what Johnnie, Mary, and Susie will get when both of them are gone.

If you draw a will alone, or if you and your wife draw separate ones together, you will come up to a moment of truth on your favorite child. Certainly Mary has been most attentive to you and loved you most. Certainly Johnnie couldn't care less about you and anyway would squander anything you left him. So perhaps Mary should get more from what you have than Johnnie.

Well, it's your money. You can leave it as you wish. But to discriminate among your children in the benefits in a will is to sow seeds of distrust in the family that may last a lifetime. Because your children are people first and children second. And those among them who were discriminated against will be inclined to suspect from now on any children who were favored. They will reason that the favored ones brainwashed the parents or used other evil tactics to gain their favors.

This is just the way things are with children and money. Believe it.

Any good lawyer you consult in drawing your will knows of the pitfalls that are recounted here. He has seen many a family squabble come through the courts as a result of wills. He will offer you the value of his experience. But he will not try to tell you what to do. It's your business.

Once you make your will, the lawyer will tell you where to

put it for safekeeping, and what should be done with it in case of death. If he's so inclined he may tell you also that a will is no more a symbol of your dying than a life insurance policy is, that most intelligent people nowadays regard a will as their most important duty from age fifty on, that in fact a will nowadays is quite a fashionable thing to talk about on the cocktail circuit.

Once your will is made, file it away. Then every three or four years, or whenever any change takes place in the circumstances surrounding the will, take it out and review it.

One final thing: If, after making your will, you move to another state, be sure to have it checked by a lawyer in that state. The differing laws among the states may require minor or major revisions in the provisions you have made. Without them, there could be difficulties in probating the will. Or the whole thing might be declared null and void. Play it safe.

Lawyers and the Income Tax

You are kidding yourself if you think you know all there is to know about the income tax laws. You know the major features, can understand the short form for your returns, and figure out what figures to put on which lines. But few people know really what benefits you can and can't get under the laws, and most of those who do are lawyers. It's their business to know, and they have the kinds of minds that were trained to understand the fine print. (Accountants are also tax experts. Your lawyer will have one on tap if needed.)

The errors a normal retired man with his reduced income would make on an income tax return would be small. The most common one, of course, is the error of paying taxes on that part of a pension which is a return of money paid into the pension plan. But there are others. A lawyer can catch them.

It might be necessary, once you retire, that you go to a lawyer only once for his advice on your return. When your retirement income has settled down and you will be having the same income and deductions each year, you can use the lawyer-approved return as a model for all the rest.

Buying and Selling Property

Any dealings with real estate are about as basic as any legal problems you will face in retirement. You may carry out such dealings without benefit of barrister and do all right. Many people have. But in an age of fast real-estate promoters and in a society where zoning, condemnations, assessments, and taxes grow always more complex it is a gamble to try it.

And the retired man is in a sorry state to gamble. He hasn't the years or the means to recoup if he's stung.

There are certain standard legal matters to be handled when you sell your home. The first is to know what you're selling. There will be a copy of your deed on file, probably in the county courthouse, and it will contain a legal description of the property. This is what counts, not the hedge at the side of the lot which you *think* is the lot line. Lot lines have a way of wandering over the years, straying as much as two or three feet in older neighborhoods.

Other standard matters include giving full details of what claims there are against your property, such as mortgages, damage suits, assessments levied by the city or county, easements granted a neighbor or the local government.

Then there are the legal mechanics, such as prorating taxes for the year in which you sell your property; getting a refund on house insurance you have paid for, and on any oil in your furnace tank; canceling the utilities and getting a refund on your water meter (if any); providing a surveyor's plot of the property you're selling and tax bills for the last two years. The lawyer will have more of these legal standard items on his list, and when he has gone through them all he may present you with the awful matter of "escrow." An escrow, in effect, is a plan whereby you put all required papers for the sale of your property into a pot.

The buyer puts all monies required for the purchase in the same pot. When everything is in, neutral parties dive in and hand each his own. The deal is closed.

These mechanics of the law will sound simple to lawyers and to retired people who have frequently bought and sold property. But the normal retired man has probably owned only one home in his lifetime, and has gone through this frustrating circus only once. He had better be smart, or he had better have a lawyer.

What has been said thus far on real-estate legalities would confront you in either buying or selling property. But there are particular legal angles to either buying or selling.

In selling, your major concern must be—assuming you have been honest all along—to make sure the deal is final. With no comebacks. No later lawsuits. In some communities the prevailing idea may be that of "buyer beware." In others it may be that of the buyer having a legal right to what he "thinks" he is buying. In still others the situation gets all confused over the issue of whether the seller knew, or didn't know, of certain defaults in the house or property.

As an example, if you sell your home and a year later termites show up in the beams, are you liable because you didn't treat the beams for termites? Or did you know they were there without telling?

The buyer of a house would like to hold you accountable for any defaults he finds after he takes over the premises. This is natural. It is also natural that if the buyer has a lawyer in on the deal that lawyer will try to include a paragraph in the sales agreement holding you accountable. Again you had better be smart, or you had better have a lawyer who can spot such a paragraph and kill it. After all, what you want is to get your money and be done with the property. The first is no particular problem; the second may take some legal footwork.

In buying a home, your legal problems are a bit more complex. In general, you will want to be buying a home that is what it seems to be, that you will have a clear deed to, that you can sell, borrow money on, will to your children, just as with any other unencumbered private asset you might hold.

This is not so simple as it ought to be. For instance, you buy a house in a new subdivision and the local real-estate taxes on it are $150. Did the promoter of this subdivision make a political deal whereby the taxes would remain low until all the houses were sold and then two years later raised to $350? This would be difficult to determine, but a local lawyer would be more likely to know than you would.

The house you buy may be on the lip of some superhighway a planner is dreaming up in Washington or the state capital. It may be in the middle of an area that may soon be condemned for a shopping center. It may be a candidate for rezoning into a business area. It may already be zoned so that you would never be able to take a roomer or renter into your house.

You could possibly buy a house on land in which you do not get the mineral rights. Which you might think is okay since you don't want to mine coal there, but which might allow somebody someday to come put an oil well in your living room.

There are many angles to this. Some of them, of course, could never be guarded against. A good legal mind advising you on the sort of deed you get can guard you against the most flagrant ones.

Now, Think for a Moment

In the legal matters already cited and in those to come you had better realize that you are in an odd position if you get into trouble. If you were a young father with three babies and an innocent face, any court or arbitrator would be inclined to lean over backward to help you in a legal dispute. If you were a senile old man, a pregnant woman, or a fellow with one leg you would ride a sympathy wave. But, after all, you are a sixty-five-year-old man who has had a chance to learn many things, and you don't look like a fool, so "For goodness' sake why were you so stupid?"

Marriage in the Later Years

This is a delicate business. It is very much legal business also. Presumably people past sixty don't marry with stars in their eyes and sex on their minds. For deep respect perhaps, for companionship, for convenience, for many things. But seldom for emotion. And seldom without money figuring prominently in the picture. The legal problems involved, which should be worked out before the preacher starts his show, include:

● A written pledge of security for the wife if she has given up a job, her Social Security, and any other means of livelihood in order to marry;

● A written agreement on how both husband and wife will contribute any private funds each has to the marriage;

● A pact or some such understanding on how each will dispose of what asset each has after death—to children, to each other, to the church, etc.

● A pact or some such understanding on how both the husband and wife will protect each other, in case one dies, from the insults and demands of the other's children, since most retired people who marry are widows or widowers with children. Often children who parade the ghosts of "our dear departed mother" or "dear old dad" can make life almost unbearable for the survivor of a gray-haired marrige.

Trust Funds . . . or Distrust Funds

Trust funds are set up by retired people for several different reasons. To get a break on taxes. To insure continuation of the family's financial status. To make Papa a big shot. To make both Papa and Mama look very, very upper class indeed in the chit-chat at the country club as they drop tidbits about "our trust fund."

But in the main, retired people set up trust funds because they don't trust their heirs to spend the money properly. Which is how the "distrust" gag comes in.

And trust funds, like so many other things, are legal matters.

In broad terms, a trust fund is a device whereby you can give a bank, say, $50,000 with instructions that after you die it pay $500 a year to your three children, for a total of $1,500 a year. (This is based on 3 percent interest. Banks, which are always conservative, are especially so on trust funds. A 3 percent return, after the bank's fee is paid, is a pretty good return. You may get more.)

Most larger banks have trust departments, where the trust funds are managed. In some areas these trust departments can handle your trust fund desires across the desk. In others the trust department will hardly talk to you at all until you bring your personal lawyer into the picture. In either case, it's a legal matter.

In the example given above, your three children would get their $500 a year for their lifetimes if the trust fund agreement reads that way. And it would be about as secure as any arrangement on money you could make. But if one of your children comes up against a grave personal crisis, such as needing $5,000 to rush a baby to Rochester for medical aid, your child would have to come ask the trustees of the trust fund for the money. And make a good case for it. Just as your widow, if you had left a trust fund for her, would have to justify any appeal for extra cash if she wanted to have a couple of weeks in private in Jamaica with a young boyfriend.

The legal angles of a trust fund are not so much in the setting up of one. Everything will be correct and proper, down to the last whereas, or the bank wouldn't touch it. The angles lie instead in the ramifications, whether or not the trust fund will provide over the long pull, while you recline out in the cemetery under a piece of marble, all that is best for the people you seek to benefit. And whether—ironically—the trust fund is going to make your beneficiaries love you or curse you.

Trust funds, if you have lots of money, can usually cut the taxes on what you leave behind. Again, it's a legal maneuver.

141

Other Business in the Bank

You and your wife or husband have a joint checking account in the bank. That's a legal problem if one of you dies. You have a safety deposit box at the bank. A legal problem. You have a joint savings account. Ditto.

In some states, in some smaller banks, and in some circumstances a husband or wife would simply take over a joint checking account if the other died. The same with a safety deposit box and a savings account.

BUT YOU CAN'T ALWAYS DO THIS. No matter what they told you down at Joe's Service Station.

Two problems can rise to haunt you: taxes, and any legal obligations of the deceased. So many different practices are in effect on these matters that nobody except the bank where you have your accounts and your safety box can tell you exactly what will happen in your case. The more common things that can happen are these:

• Tax authorities can freeze the two accounts and the safety deposit box until they make an appraisal of them to determine the tax liability of the one who died.

• The bank itself **can** freeze everything in order to protect itself in case anybody has a legal claim against the deceased.

• Court officials can issue orders to tie up the accounts because of provisions made in a will or because of debts incurred by the deceased.

• The bank can allow the survivor to have access to one-half the checking and savings accounts, meanwhile freezing the deceased's half.

All of these, you will note, are directed against the deceased and not the survivor, but when ownership is joint the survivor is stuck with the problem. Which means you can't even die without a lawyer.

There are usually ways to set up checking and savings accounts so that the death of a husband or wife will not hamper the survivor in obtaining his or her rightful money. Only a local lawyer or the local banker can explain how. Some husbands, figuring they will be the first to die, avoid the whole commotion by setting up a private savings account for their wives, of about $500, to tide them over any freeze on their joint holdings.

A safety deposit box that is held jointly has about the same problems the checking and savings accounts have. Except what's in the box can turn out to be a can of legal worms. Stocks, bonds, deeds, etc., resting there in joint ownership, can be worded in half a dozen different ways: as joint ownership, as tenants in common, as joint tenants with rights of survivorship, as tenants by the entirety, and other mumbo-jumbo. All these mean different things to different states and different judges.

A careful study of the laws governing such things in the particular state where you live, or a visit to a lawyer or banker, can guide you in the proper wording to use for joint ownership and thus save your survivor some taxes and some bother.

Just to worry you a bit further, very little of what has been said here will apply to you if you live in what is called a community property state, or move to one. California is a community property state. So is Texas. Broadly speaking, such a state decrees that everything acquired in a marriage is half the wife's and half the husband's.

This is long enough to remain in the stuffy atmosphere of a bank.

A Family Friend

A retired couple has a serious need of a family friend, not somebody to play rook or sip tea with, but a man of integrity who knows the family affairs and has affection enough to step in and help when a crisis comes.

A banker or a lawyer would properly fit this role, and of the two the lawyer might be best. Make a friend of one.

It would be wise of you to choose one who is younger than you by maybe fifteen years. You want him around when you grow too old to act on your own and when you die. You want him around to counsel the survivor.

A lawyer who is a family friend can give you much legal counsel that you would not get otherwise, because most of the family problems you come to face would seem to you embarrassing if you presented them to a lawyer you did not know well. For instance, you want to build an apartment on to your son's home and live there. Or you want to put up $5,000 to add to the down payment of a son who wants to buy a house, and move in with him. You would mention such things to a family friend, but hardly take them up with an impersonal lawyer. And the family friend would quickly remind you of the grave legal risks you are taking, since any worth you add to somebody else's real-estate title you may eventually have to kiss good-bye.

You would tell a family friend of serious reservations you have about the reliability of the man who is married to your daughter. Your pride wouldn't let you tell anybody else. The friend could tell you how you might arrange your money so that the daughter got exclusive rights to it in her name.

You would tell a family friend that, as a husband, you were apprehensive about leaving all you have to your wife—which you want to do—because she would probably shower her bounty on her favorite of the three children. You could learn how to side-step this danger.

You, as a husband, would be willing to let a family friend step in and take charge of things if sudden death left your wife a widow. You would have faith that he would do and advise properly. You would not grant such a privilege to an impersonal lawyer. And you'd better not grant it to any well-meaning neighbors or to your children.

Finally, every retired couple should have a "Whom to Inform in Case of Emergency." Your children would be all right for this. So would an impersonal lawyer. But best of all would be a lawyer who is a family friend. If you traveled abroad and landed in a foreign jail, if you went out of town for the weekend and your house burned, if you were sued for money, if you and your wife were killed in an auto accident, the family lawyer would know what to do or whom to notify. His office can be the depository of papers that make sense of your affairs—where to find an extra key to the house if you are out of town, which child to call in case of illness, where the money is kept, who the family doctor is, and under what tree in the backyard you've hidden the twenty-dollar gold pieces.

Now you've got to work out a way to pay the family friend for these legal services he gives you. Family friendship doesn't go *that* far. And a box of cookies next Christmas won't quite do it. The lawyer, even if your friend, has to live. And he has to pay a secretary to type all those unreadable legal papers he draws up.

Just a Minute, Now

Except in the case of a devoted family friend, as just related, and in a few other situations, a lawyer is a man of the law. Nothing more. Many of them would like you to believe they are all things to all men. You have legal problems frequently as you move into retirement. Don't let the guy at the feed store tell you how to handle them. Go to a lawyer. By the same token, if you have financial affairs, go to a banker or an investment counselor or a broker, not to a lawyer. If you have medical problems, go to a doctor. If you have problems with your children, go to the pastor of your church or to a family counselor.

Wrapping It Up

It should be emphasized that in all probability you will go through your retirement without having to call on a lawyer, except for a few matters such as wills. You aren't going to be having street fights, divorces, and sojourns in jail. Many people never set eyes on a lawyer after reaching sixty-five. But the retirement years have legal problems that are peculiarly their own, and a lawyer is a good thing to have around.

Choosing a lawyer, if you don't know one, is fairly simple.

Almost every county has its own bar association, composed usually of the better lawyers in the area. Phone the association, state your needs, and make your choice from the names given you. Or you can take the recommendations of friends.

Or you can watch the newspapers to see which lawyers are most prominent in civic affairs. You probably won't need a specialized lawyer, but a general practitioner. You can choose a tax expert if you have lots of money, or a trial lawyer if you plan to steal a lot. You can choose—and some people like to do this—a lawyer with political leanings. He will frequently have influence in certain quarters that could help you. He might be a good avenue to a political job, if you want one. On the other hand, he may get elected to something and be away at the state capital the next time you get in trouble.

Lawyers in the main are honorable men, though there are some scalawags among them. Your chances of picking an honorable one, especially outside the larger cities, are quite good. But they are an argumentative lot. And they have a yen for objecting. Show this book to one lawyer and he'll object to half that's in it. Take it down the street to another one and he'll tell you that that half is quite okay and then object to the other half.

TEN

———◡———

USING YOUR LEISURE

You had just as well face up, in the beginning, to the truth about your leisure in retirement. You're not going to like what you see. You may not even believe it.

But your retirement will be far better if you'll face up to it.

Your retirement, while a baptism of sorts, is not going to change your soul or your heart. You are going to be just as dumb and just as smart as you were before. Just as lazy and just as efficient. Just as mean and just as gracious. In brief you're going to be the same person . . . with time added.

Now, if you didn't find time to read books before retirement, you won't afterward. You can be fairly well assured, unless you're freakish, that you found more time for leisure activities while on the job than you are going to find in retirement.

Strange? Indeed it is. Which is why you may not believe it.

The explanation for this, until a better one comes along, is that you are an organized person in your working years. In your leisure you aren't, and your days go all to pieces.

Haven't you been hearing all these assertions by retired people that their days are so full "I just can't find time to do all the things I want to do"? They aren't fibbing. They believe it. Because in their unorganized state they are stretching forty-five minutes of work into an eight-hour day.

147

Don't let these words discourage you. There are some magnificent ways to use your leisure and they will be coming up shortly. But first it is good for you to know that once you go into retirement you must be prepared to fight the narcotic that leisure is.

Here is a day in the life of a man after about a year in retirement. It is fairly typical. Study it carefully, because it is the sort of thing you want to avoid.

7 A.M.—Got out of bed. Donned a robe, went outside to get the newspaper, rummaged around the kitchen until his wife appeared. Looked over paper while wife prepared breakfast. Ate leisurely with one cup of coffee. Then took second cup and newspaper into the living room to watch television until nine.

9 to 10 A.M.—Dressed and shaved. Put away yesterday's clothes. Helped wife make the bed. Took out the trash. Tried television to see if anything different had come on.

10 A.M.—Went out to mow the lawn. Pulled power mower out of the shed and found it was out of gas. Checked the oil and in the process found the blade had three bad nicks in it. Decided it was a good time to sharpen the blade since the mower was out of gas and could be turned over on its back. Went to his tool bench for a file. Tried it and found it too worn to do the job. Decided he'd have to drive to town before he could do the mowing, both for gas and a new file. Got a rag and wiped off the mower. Walked out to front yard, kicking dandelions with his heel on the way. Got into conversation with foreman of street-cleaning crew.

11:30 A.M.—Back into the house. Found wife had to go to the church to deliver some materials to the president of the Women's Society. He'd drive her.

12:30 P.M.—Lunch. Made another check of television to see if anything different had come on. Found a program that wasn't bad. A movie . . . cowboys.

2 P.M.—A nap.

3:30 P.M.—Considered making four calls on neighbors for the Community Chest Drive which he had promised to do. Decided evening calls would be better. Wrote a check for the telephone bill. Figured he had better drive downtown and mail it.

148

Forgot the gas can, but decided it was too late anyway to mow the lawn today.

4:30 P.M.—Surveyed the property. Picked some lettuce out of the vegetable garden and brought it into the house, washed it, wrapped it in waxed paper, put it in the refrigerator. Went back outside to pull grass from around the zinnias.

5:30 P.M.—Told his wife they should get their daily exercise and took her for a walk around the neighborhood, casing each yard to see if it had lettuce or zinnias as good as his.

6:30 P.M.—Dinner preparations, while he set the table.

7:00 P.M.—Television. Decided Community Chest calls could wait.

8:00 P.M.—Television.

9:00 P.M.—Television and a dish of ice cream.

10:00 P.M.—Television.

10:45 P.M.—Television. Took shoes off.

11:00 P.M.—To bed.

Don't laugh. Whether you are a man or a woman, don't laugh. And don't doubt. This is a typical day in the life of many retired people who were going to raise a cloud of dust the moment they retired and got their freedom.

You should know it. It is negative. It is discouraging. But you must realize that the leisure that comes to you with retirement is, first of all, a narcotic. You must whip it.

Plan Ahead

The best way to keep yourself from sliding into a do-nothing retirement state is first to define the general areas of leisure-time activities, then choose the ones you want, and finally make some advance preparations.

There are ten general areas of leisure activity where retired people have found satisfaction. This chapter will cover them.

1. A PART-TIME JOB. There are gray-haired jobs available, many of them part-time, many of them at such odd hours as midnight to 6 A.M. A man or woman can find these jobs in almost

any community except the small town. But seldom through the usual channels of want ads and employment agencies. They must make their search on information supplied by friends, through business contacts left over from the old job, and by persistent personal calls on likely employers.

If a part-time job is what you want, you should look primarily to an establishment that is small, that has no labor unions, that has no pension plan. It might be a young construction firm, a neighborhood store, a motel, a lumberyard, a nursery, automobile sales agency. Look at the classified section of your phone book and you can find hundreds of them.

Don't expect the jobs to be glamorous. Don't expect them to be jobs as good as the one you have retired from. And don't be surprised at the low pay. There are very few fine jobs for retired people, despite what you may have heard.

The great virtue of a part-time job is that it lets you eat your cake and have it, too. You can work four hours a day, or three days a week, and have both activity and leisure. Another virtue of it is that it will add to your retirement income.

2. HOBBIES.   Hobbies could be, but aren't, a significant factor in the lives of people now retiring. There is a popular notion abroad in the country that retirement is one vast hobbyland and that if a man or woman can just have a few butterfly nets and a little clay for pot-making everything will be taken care of.

Retired people aren't finding it so.

The reason, as you can appreciate with a little reflection, is that most hobbies are a bit too trivial for a person who has been out in the business world fighting dragons for a living. You won't find them offensive. You may want to take a turn at oil painting, at collecting stones, at model trains, but you'll find they aren't absorbing enough to hold your interest for long.

You may also find that you're slightly gun-shy at just the mention of the word "hobbies." Too many silly people are doing silly things with them. The image of the word is not good, at least to mature people.

Yet the activities gathered under the name of hobbies are many and wondrous. You can mold a fine retirement out of some

150

of them. All you have to do is add a little muscle to them and make them meaningful.

You can make them meaningful by making some money out of them. Or by becoming professional enough to draw attention to yourself, to be interviewed by the newspapers, to be invited to give lectures. Or by involving yourself so thoroughly in your particular hobby that you are drawn into the hobby societies, the hobby shows, and the various affairs sponsored by the hobby trade.

You can accomplish any of these without much trouble. In fact, you can accomplish all three at once, as a retired telephone man, S. W. Jordan, did at his home in Pennsylvania.

Four months out into retirement Mr. Jordan found time hanging heavy, and at the urging of his wife began looking around for some sort of hobby that would interest him. He went browsing one afternoon in a nearby hobby shop. Most cities now have hobby shops or have hardware stores and drugstores with hobby departments.

Mr. Jordan came to a shelf that was given over to various types of liquid plastics and resins which could be molded into figurines, dominoes, ashtrays, etc. They could also be used to make a clear, hard surface for a coffee table. Mr. Jordan wondered if he might not buy about three dollars' worth of different-colored United States postage stamps, lay them over the top of a table he had at home, then cover them with one of these plastic products. It would make a colorful and interesting table, and it ought to work.

It worked. And the comments of friends who came in were most pleasing.

Next came some foreign coins the Jordans had collected over the years. They were placed in circles on a round table top, with a rare United States silver dollar in the center. The liquid plastic that covered them was just over a fourth-inch deep, and when it hardened the coins looked as if they were under glass. Three roses pressed on a small mahogany board came next, followed by color prints, prized photographs, thin pieces of antique jewelry. All were placed on boards of fine woods. All were covered by coats of plastic thick enough to preserve them permanently.

151

"It wasn't all child's play to get started," Mr. Jordan said. "I made some awful messes. I ruined a few treasures. But I got absorbed enough with the idea to follow it through properly.

"When some of the plastic began to wrinkle as it hardened, I wrote the manufacturer and asked for advice on how to correct it. I got a fistful of literature back. When I had difficulty building a retaining wall around the edge of a table in order to pour in the plastic, I wrote another manufacturer. I got suggestions ranging from metal linoleum strips to aluminum foil. I began building a library shelf on this comparatively new hobby—or is it art?"

Mr. Jordan got attention. First from neighbors, then from his local newspaper, and as a result of the publicity, from local clubs looking for an interesting speaker. Eventually he was placing some of his own "art" pieces in gift shops, and was accepting fees to enshrine other people's treasures on their own table tops.

"I soon had to move my operation out of the kitchen, as you might imagine," Mr. Jordan said. "I'm now set up in the corner of our basement with a liquid-plastic workshop that would make Du Pont envious."

A Mr. John M. Fellows did with a camera hobby about what Mr. Jordan did with plastics. He built a darkroom in his basement, and began spending so much money on equipment he decided he had better get some of it back. He spent forty dollars for cards saying he would photograph children "as they've never been shown before." He mailed the cards to families in the better sections of town. He got their names out of the phone book. Mr. Fellows' proposition was that he would come to the home when the children were playing, would hide nearby and get shots of the children when they were being their most natural selves. While the commercial photographers in his town who had never thought of anything but formal portraits of children wondered what had happened to their business, Mr. Fellows was making friends. having fun, and counting the profit.

Leslie Henderson had a loving wife who gave him a fine woodworking set, including power saw and drill, when he retired. After he had made bookshelves, flower boxes, and picnic tables for half the neighborhood, he began teaching a class in "Home

152

Carpentry" at an adult education school. Walter Guthrie went in for lapidary (cutting and polishing native stones to make jewelry, etc.). He became an expert. The geology department of his state government hired him as a consultant to classify stones in the state that would be appropriate for his specialty.

In a nutshell, what these stories say is that a hobby is a fine deal for retirement if you don't make it a hobby—that is, some casual plaything to pick up and tinker with when you grow bored. You have to work at it. The satisfaction you get out of it will just about balance the thought you give to it.

3. FISHING AND GOLF. Fishing and golf are the retirement twins, both always associated with the delights of age sixty-five. They aren't hobbies, in the usual sense, and if you think so watch a fisherman sitting for four hours in the sun and catching nothing, or a golfer making a bonehead shot on the eighteenth hole. They are hard and serious work.

Fishing and golf are retirement affairs mostly of men. Most men like one or both of them. Most men never get quite enough of each during their working years, and, like the country boy who could have only one ice-cream cone a week, they yearn for the grand day when they can indulge themselves every day.

They find it is not quite the fun they expected. There is opportunity for too much of it, for one thing. And men invariably grow sated with anything they get too much of.

Having seen the piers in Florida lined with retired fishermen, you may be inclined to doubt this. But if you had a choice of only fishing or shuffleboard, wouldn't *you* rather fish?

A scarcity of companions is a major handicap on both fishing and golf. On an ocean pier a retired man can nearly always run into a crony; it is actually a good place for him to make new friends. But if he must do his fishing on a lake or river, it is not easy to find a companion to go along. Old friends at the company are working, except on the weekend. Retired friends have to drive their wives somewhere, can't afford it, or don't feel like it.

Golf is much the same. Old friends back at the company who played golf with you on weekends and holidays tend to play with co-workers who are still on the job. From Monday through

Friday when the retired man can have ready access to a golf course he frequently must go alone or not at all.

You should also consider, if you plan to make golf a major part of your retirement, that it is costly. Lost balls and greens fees are not small items in a retirement budget. Fishing is cheaper, except that a fisherman grows tired of catching only bream in his local waters and longs for some trout casting in a distant mountain stream. Money again.

Suggestions on getting companions: If you play golf at a country club, tell the manager you would like to organize a small group for weekday rounds. Tell the manager at any public course the same. Both would like to see the golf course used more on weekdays and less on weekends and will probably put you in touch with companions. Fishing companions are harder to come by, but if you will spend some time around a sports shop that sells fishing equipment, or around a place that sells bait or rents boats, you will eventually meet some playmates.

4. SOCIAL ACTIVITY. The rich frequently devote their retirement exclusively to social activities. The yacht harbors of California and Florida and the villas along the Riviera are the best examples of this. They play, seek out new forms of pleasure, spend money freely, and while there are sometimes signs that they grow jaded, they stay with it. Apparently it brings them happiness. At least it brings them admiration from a lot of people who would like to be in on it.

Social activity can be an important and satisfying leisure-time life for those on a lesser financial and social plane. If you like people, just for themselves, you can—with effort—make a wide circle of social friends when you retire. With these friends you can arrange activities that your budget can afford.

Understand that a set of social friends does not come full-blown. You build it, couple by couple. It may take a year or so.

Start your building only after you get firmly in your mind just what you are looking for—social friends. And since you no longer have a job to tend, you want social friends who can be active on weekdays as well as on weekends, and in daytime as well as in the evening. This narrows your choices down somewhat, primarily to other retired couples, and among these you want to choose, if you can, couples (1) who are not too infirm to go out in the evening; (2) who are financially able to afford the modest social activities you want; and (3) who can drive a car; and (4) who like people.

But don't confine your choices exclusively to retired people. Look for some couples who are still active and in the fifties. Even cultivate a couple or so who are still in their forties. You need some permanence in your social life as the older friends begin fading from the picture.

You build your social set simply. You just start. Pick the dullest time of the week, which will probably be about five o'clock on a Sunday afternoon, and invite about six couples to your house for a hamburger-lemonade supper. Don't start out on alcohol; even if you and your guests like it, most retirement budgets can't afford it.

The six couples need not be, and probably shouldn't be, people you know well. You're expanding . . . see? You need have no concern about people you know slightly turning down your invitation. Just about anybody will be glad to go just about anywhere at five o'clock on a Sunday. If it's free.

Once your guests are assembled, start asking them questions about themselves, but discreetly. What do they do for pleasure? Whom do they know? Where do they go? How do they live? Before your party is over you will know who among the six couples have promise as social friends.

Those among your guests who are socially inclined will follow up your party with an invitation for you to come to their homes. Unless they decided you are freaks. If these return invitations do not come in about three weeks, then deliberately violate the etiquette rules and invite two or three of the promising couples back to your house, say, in the evening to play bridge, to make candy for children, or to see color slides, with lemonade or coffee and some cookies.

You must realize that people are generally socially lazy, and thus you should feel no embarrassment in inviting them at least three times before they honor you with an invitation. If they come, they like you.

Now, out of the six couples who ate your Sunday hamburgers maybe only one or two will pan out as social friends of the future. This would be about normal. But you start building on these. They have friends you haven't met, but will in time. They have discovered social activities you haven't, but now will. And through the new friends' friends you will come to know the friends' friends' friends, and on and on. The panorama of social activities you can engage in (on a retirement budget) will grow wider and wider.

Just remember, if you think social intercourse will make your retirement good, then it must be a continuing job. You can't make six friends and quit. You must be constantly recruiting new people for your circle. And as you recruit them you must look constantly for friends who will fill the hours of your week you want filled. Tennis friends for the morning. Fishing and swimming friends for the afternoon. Luncheon friends. Monday night friends for cards or games, when television is not worth watching.

Social activities, on a scale you can afford, may be among the most rewarding things you can do in retirement. Not to be a popular kid, not to make people drop envious comments about you. But to stay mentally alive, to have something to do, and simply to enjoy people, who are more interesting, and often funnier, than monkeys.

5. CIVIC AFFAIRS. You owe something in the area of civic affairs. Perhaps you should plan to pay.

It is possible for you to get some handsome returns, and this will depend almost entirely on how hard you work at it.

Civic affairs, which include clubs and do-good organizations, are a peculiar animal in our times. With some notable exceptions, the workers in civic affairs are dedicated primarily to advancing themselves, not to advancing the civic project in hand. They will want to carry the project to a successful conclusion, for sure, but only incidentally for the good the project might do. Rather they seek the honor and glory that come to those who do complete such projects.

You may rest assured that you'll have something thrown at you if you make such a charge as this at a civic-affairs luncheon. But in general the charge is true, and it is good that you understand just where the motivations lie if you delve into civic affairs.

Lawyers are usually very active in civic affairs, getting the presidency of this, the chairmanship of that, or heading up some fund campaign. Not because they have any more civic zeal than anybody else, but because they want to build a reputation and meet prospective clients. Rising young men in large companies are always giving the lawyers a run for their glory because they can get their picture in the paper through civic affairs and this might help advance the career. Also because large companies like to be publicly identified with good civic works and encourage their employees to get with it.

There are other traditional types in civic affairs—the frustrated businessman seeking honors he can't get from business, ambitious women trying to prove a point, and people trying to broaden their business and personal contacts.

Get into the swim with these people. You can keep in touch with a moving world, make friends, and accomplish much that is good. Just be content to be another nice fellow named George who sits at the corner table at luncheons and serves on the membership committee. Or be prepared to cross swords with the eager beavers who are struggling for the titles. If you should decide to fight it out, you will have one major advantage: you have plenty of time to give to a civic project; the eager beavers still have a job to master.

6. WELFARE WORK. Welfare work is also a peculiar animal, but with satisfaction you can get nowhere else in your retirement.

Welfare organizations, as you know, are becoming major industries. Professionals have taken them over, and many of these professionals are women. They do things in a manner that sometimes seems very strange to a man or woman who has spent a lifetime in business. Committee meetings, seminars, panel talks, briefings, reports, surveys, more committee meetings, and on and on.

The retired person volunteering to work for one of these welfare organizations usually has no role in the professional councils. He or she will be stuffing envelopes or counting the committees while the professionals buzz along upstairs.

Still, the cause is good. The tasks are not unpleasant. And always there will be other retired people who volunteered as you did and will be around for conversation and friendship. There might always come a day when, if you volunteered, you would be chosen to direct one of the front committees in a fund campaign. And get your picture in the paper. But a retired person shouldn't bank on it.

7. TRAVEL.   If you have money to spare when you retire, you are going on some travels, whether you have fun or not. If you don't have the money, you aren't. Retirement travel is about as simple as that.

If you don't have the money, there's no point in kidding yourself. Travel is glamorous, it's educational, and it has interest and excitement to it. If you can't afford it, get it off your mind and go fishing. But hear this: Travel in retirement has not turned out to be too satisfying. By age sixty-five the comforts of home are very dear. The body is not too flexible. The eyes grow tired. Since most retirement travel is by automobile, men and their wives have found long trips an almost unbearable trap of sixty-mile-an-hour concrete. And constant tension. There are few little towns to see anymore—they got bypassed—and there is little scenery. The motels, the gasoline stations, the snack bars, all seem to have come out of the same mail-order catalogue.

It is just not the fun it would have been at age forty-five. It is not the fun retired people would have found in a slower age. So you'll find they don't go on many travels before they start giving excuses for not going. Travel becomes an occasional incident and not a major factor in the use of retirement leisure.

8. GOING TO SCHOOL.   For people now going into retirement, one of the greatest blessings since Congress gaiters and mustard plasters is going to school.

158

Education has become fashionable. It has moved up just under Motherhood and the Flag in the list of our noblest words. As a result, a retired person can hardly walk down the street without bumping into it.

As a pursuit for retirement it holds a promise that few other activities do; it points onward and upward and will lead, if you let it, to some interest that will hold you all the way through your golden years.

Here is how today's retired people can, and do, capitalize on the great boom that has come in education:

- In university graduate schools. Those who took a B.S. or B.A. degree in their younger years can recover their credits from the institution where they got them and enroll in the graduate schools of good universities all over the country to specialize. They can get a master's degree in whatever subject they want. A master's degree, taking maybe two years, is a fine recommendation for a job even at age sixty-seven.

- In university undergraduate schools. Persons who finished only high school, or became dropouts in college, can pick up where they left off and wind up with a college degree. Starting from scratch, it normally takes four years.

- In university evening schools. These are operated pretty much as the regular undergraduate school. But there are more adults in the classrooms. Some give credits toward a degree. Some don't.

- In "auditing." In many of the three types of schools a person can enroll in classes of his choice as an "auditor," usually paying a fee that is less than tuition, taking no exams, and getting no credits. He or she just sits and listens to what knowledge is being dispensed. Many retired people find this the most appealing of the lot.

- In adult education classes. These are conducted all over by various organizations. Every city has them, sometimes under auspices of the YMCA, sometimes under the city school system. These classes may or may not lead to credits toward a college degree. In the main they are

159

concerned more with trades or handicrafts. Many retired people attend them.

Adult education classes and the "auditing" of college courses are most popular with today's retired people for an obvious reason: most of them never went to college and don't care to get involved with that level of education. The person retiring today at sixty-five came up to college age about 1922. Not many people could afford college then. Or they were serving in the army, or they were helping Ma and Pa out on the farm.

So, if you go in for education in retirement, don't be bashful. The fellow sitting next to you in the classroom may never have finished high school either. And furthermore, he looks older and uglier than you do.

9. POLITICS.   Politics is what they call seasonal work except for a few professionals who tend the store between elections. But when it is in season, it is one of the significant uses you can make of your leisure.

In your working years you probably have not been entirely free to get involved in political matters. To engage too prominently in a political fight might have put you in opposing camps to your boss or your company, and might have been irritation all around if it was against company policy for employees to become involved in public controversy.

Once you retire, you are free of these limitations. Nobody is going to take your pension away, or your Social Security . . . and don't let anybody tell you so.

There are several specific advantages you can reap if you become involved in politics. For one thing you can get fighting mad in a political campaign, and this is good for you occasionally. You can become completely absorbed in it, forgetting to take out the trash at home and sometimes forgetting to eat. This is good for you occasionally, too. On a more tangible level, politics offers you a chance to stand for, and fight for, what you believe in. From taxes to foreign policy, from the state highway program to city garbage collections, you can be a force for good or bad. Nowhere else can you be quite so strong a force. Of course you can write letters to newspapers, tell your children that they had

160

better vote and your neighbors how they ought to. But if you want your ideas, your influence, your personality, to be felt, get actively into a political camp you believe in and speak your convictions.

You can make many friends in a political campaign, some of whom will last a lifetime. You can also make lifetime enemies. You can win a good political job, for two years, four years, or longer if you work for a candidate and he wins. You can devote all your time, and a good bit of your personal money, to a campaign for three months and wind up with a crushed spirit. These are the breaks of the game. But if you lose, there is always another campaign coming up in a couple of years, and then you can get even madder.

In general you will fare best if you get into politics through one of the two established parties, Democratic or Republican. You will have a far richer experience if you get into a state campaign as against a county or city campaign. It's just as easy, and from there, next time, you can move into a national race.

You can make your entry into politics through the precinct chairman of the party you chose, or through the county chairman, or the state chairman. Any of them will put you to work at something. But your best bet may be to pick a candidate you like in a primary campaign, and go directly to him to offer your services. In this way you become a worker for a man instead of a party, and your breaks can be better this way. If the man wins, you can be sure the party will want you around. Of course, when you pick a horse in a primary, you have two chances to lose—in both the primary and the general election. But if your man comes through all this and wins, oh, boy! In retirement you can afford this sort of gamble.

Don't go into politics if you expect to be paid a salary every week for your work. There are better jobs. Go in as a volunteer. This will make you a big frog instead of a little one when rewards are passed out . . . if your candidate wins.

10. YOUR OWN PRIVATE WAY. While people contribute most of your happiness, as you go through life, they also contribute most of your grief. It may well be that once your pension

comes, you will want to be rid of associates, of bosses, of rules, of somebody else's game. There are some delightful roads open to you if you do.

Some of the happiest retired people, without question, are those who have devoted their leisure to some personal project which they can carry out more or less in private, when and as they want, and have the satisfaction of making their own mistakes. Each man or woman must decide what this personal project will be, based on the particular retirement circumstances and particular interests. But here are some such projects that may give you an idea:

A STUDY OF YOUR FAMILY HISTORY. The fancy name for this is genealogy, which is enough to frighten you off. Just set out to find where your Grandpa came from, and why. And how he made his money. Genealogy will slide quietly into the picture as you go along, because once you start tracing the fascinating story of one man's family—yours—you will likely become so absorbed you'll never stop.

A STUDY OF THE YEAR IN WHICH YOU WERE BORN. Some people who have retired in recent years have become so involved in this project, once they started it, that they have become authorities on "a year" in their community or state and are asked to give lectures and write articles for local newspapers and historical magazines. A particular dividend of the project is that everybody in sight who is your same age will start coming around to contribute to your lore.

A SEARCH FOR ANTIQUES. Despite all the searches of recent years there are still great treasures in antiques tucked back in the smokehouses and attics of old homes. When you retire, you have more time than anybody to roam the countryside, become acquainted with the occupants of old houses, and gain access to the "junk" that no longer interests them. This project will lead you to the study of antique books, which you'll like, and, if you're good, to friendships with antique dealers and perhaps to a shop of your own.

WRITING. You'll not reach age sixty-five without having a story you want to tell unless you're a freak. The most satisfying way to tell it is to write it. That's also the most profitable way. Writing is no mystery, and it is not difficult if you know high-school English. All you have to do is *sit down and do it.* You'll need a typewriter. You can master it. What you are reading here was written by hunt-and-peck, with two fingers, which is the only system the author has used in thirty years of writing.

COLLECTING. Anything from doorknobs to carriage wheels.

Postscript: Remember now, when you retire, you put your financial affairs on a monthly instead of a weekly basis, and at the same time you go on a seven-day week instead of a five-day one. You don't have any days off anymore. So, in making the most of your leisure, get away from the five-day concept and lay your plans for a solid week.

~~~

ELEVEN

WAYS TO INCREASE YOUR INCOME

There are lots of ways to increase your income. And they're easier than you've been led to believe.

Your initial step is to appreciate two facts:

1. You are not a normal income-maker.
2. The activity from which you make your income is not normal. Both you and it are out of the pattern of the American economic machine.

You are at an age when society thinks you should rest and when you rate no card in the files of employment agencies. Or else you are a sleeping genius who has held a job all these years in order to eat and who now, with freedom and eating money secured, can flower into something significant. So you're bad or you're good, but you aren't normal. The activity from which you will make your income divides about the same way—bad and lowly or dramatic and good.

If you are one of those who have nursed a dream through all these years, if there is some particular work or achievement you could put your heart and soul into, but haven't because you had to cling to the security of your job, then you are the type who can amass a small fortune in retirement. You will need some money, and you will need some nerve. The money you can probably get. The nerve you've got or you haven't

Here is how three men have amassed substantial money after retiring from what at best were ordinary jobs:

A certain Mr. Brown was in love with trailers. He had been for years. Bounding off down the open road with a trailer hitched to the back of his car was to him the most romantic adventure a man could have. And what marvelous construction, he thought, with everything built in, neat, convenient, and economical. Mr. Brown just couldn't see why everybody wouldn't want to live in a trailer. So, he got a hefty mortgage on his home, borrowed all he could on his life insurance policies, pushed his credit, and set up a sales lot for mobile homes near a giant new industrial development in the Midwest. He hit the jackpot.

A Mr. Watson, who had spent his working years in an office, was a frustrated builder. He had always had a yen to build houses, small cottages, shacks, stores, anything. And through the years he had played with tools and dreamed over designs. He retired, moved to Florida, built a small clever cottage which he sold at a profit. He built two more, made a profit. From there he moved in full-scale on the housebuilding boom.

Then there was Mr. Thompson. He had always yearned to be a boss. Boss of anything would do, just so long as he could run things as he thought they ought to be run. He sized up the local trucking facilities in his community, which he found deplorable, then got contracts with eight stores to handle freight shipments to the premises and deliver parcels to customers. On the basis of the contracts he was able to buy on credit enough trucks to do the job. He has been expanding and thriving ever since.

These tycoon routes to increased retirement income take nerve and money, as stated. They usually take imagination and the energy for bold, dramatic moves. You can make a lot of money. You might also keep in mind that you can fall flat on your face and lose your shirt.

The Consultant

The most glamorous of the big-money retirement activities at present is in the magic world of "consultants." You, too, can be one. Maybe.

A consultant, at the retirement level, is generally a person with particular skills, particular knowledge, or particular business contacts who can provide a large company with something it wants. The consultant can range from a man in overalls in the plant to a stuffed shirt in a private office. His or her pay can range from $100 a week for three months to $15,000 a year from now on. It depends on the special virtues of the consultant.

You might as well know that some of the most spectacular consulting jobs go to retired people whose nephews are presidents of the companies hiring them. Or to retired people owning a bundle of stock in the company. Or to executives who know where the company skeletons are hidden. Still, you can be a consultant if you have the qualifications and if you'll use your wits to sell them.

You can be a skilled toolmaker and become a consultant to a toolmaker who can't get the bugs out of his machines. You can be a smart telephone man and become a consultant to a large plant or office building trying to set up and operate an intricate phone system. You can be an experienced transportation man, with a railroad, airline, or trucking concern, and become a consultant to a manufacturer who doesn't know how to get his products distributed efficiently. You can be an automobile worker and become a consultant to a manufacturer supplying an automobile factory.

The consultant business, while quite legitimate in most cases, has its seamy side. So watch it. A company would hire you as a consultant to help itself, not because of your pretty blue eyes. Some companies, competitors of your own company, would hire you in an effort to wring from you what trade secrets it could. Beware of this, because not only would the company throw you out like an old rag when it had wrung you dry, but you would never quite feel the same again if you had betrayed your own company. Nice people don't do it.

Almost any company that hired you as a consultant would have only limited need for you. Once you had taught your skills to the company's regular employees, it would have no further reason to keep you around. Once you had solved the particular problem bothering the company, or once you had introduced the executives and salesmen to all your business contacts, why should it keep paying you?

So, if you see an opening as a consultant, make the most of it, set your price high because you can sell yourself just once, and stay honorable. Then keep the coffeepot simmering, because you'll be home soon.

With the tycoons and the consultants out of the way, you come now to the more conventional ways of increasing your retirement income. There are three primary ones: another job, hobbies, a personal business.

Another Job

The best way to get another job in retirement is to get it before you retire. You can sometimes land a good one this way. But you have to start negotiating for it up to a year before you retire. The last three weeks won't work. It is a bizarre fact, but a real one, that a man or woman who is working is interesting to business and the one who is retired or on the verge of it isn't.

An officer in a business concern or institution who does the hiring can and does regard a sixty-four-year-old who has a good job as a "fine hunk of talent" that should be captured, and then can and does regard that same person as a has-been on a pension one year later.

So if you want another job after retirement, line it up well in advance of your retirement. And while you're about it—if it's not yet too late for you—look into the possibility of taking the new job at about age 63, with a guarantee that you will not be retired when you reach age sixty-five.

Maybe you don't want to fool around with another job until you retire from your present one, or maybe it's too late now to make advance connections. What then are the openings for a has-been on a pension?

MOTELS.   The pay is fair, the hours are often from midnight to 8 A.M., and the peace and quiet are wonderful. Jobs are available in the odd hours at many motels, and the qualifications are few. Just go to a motel and apply, have an honest face, and show you have enough savvy to know that Mr. and Mrs. John Smith who want to register in at 1 A.M. aren't. Motels are plentiful, so even if you are living in a country town, so long as it is near a superhighway, you can make your pitch. If you live in a city, you have a good chance to connect with a job as night clerk in some of the many small hotels that are off the main avenues. The problems are a bit tougher here than in a motel, and the Smiths a bit more unreal.

SALESMANSHIP.   Almost any retired person can get a job in selling. Usually the only pay is commissions. Frequently the selling is door to door. Retired people are considered rather good for door-to-door work because their age tags them as harmless and they can better gain access to the living room to show their wares. In recent years firms that sell vacuum cleaners and encyclopedias, among others, have sought to recruit retired people for this work. Watch the want ads in the newspapers.

REAL ESTATE.   In communities all over the country, retired men and women are buzzing about selling houses. In most communities they have to have some minor schooling and get a license to sell. Most can pass the tests, and some make good money. It is pleasant work. The pay is usually commissions. Go have a talk with an established real-estate agent.

CLERKING.   Smaller stores in the smaller towns or on the outskirts of cities employ many retired people as clerks. Go have a look at the gray hairs behind the hardware and dry-goods counters if you don't believe it. You must look for stores that are small enough not to have a pension plan or a labor union, or any fringe benefits, or very high pay. Which is not so desirable, but that's the way things are. Still, there are jobs to be had.

TEACHING. This is an intriguing area of retirement jobs. But it has rank almost as strict as the United States Army. If you have a Ph.D. degree, you may find a teaching assignment in a university; a master's degree may earn a job in a community college or a high school; a routine B.A. or B.S. degree could secure a job in a high school. If you have none of these degrees, you can still get a teaching job: in a vocational school if you are a master of certain trades; in certain small colleges if you can lecture well on some field of specialized knowledge; in a vast range of evening schools, adult education schools, YMCA schools, etc., if you are an expert on any subject the particular school wants to teach. And in some of these schools the subjects range from pottery and butterfly-catching to electrical circuits and the mechanics of a lawnmower. Go to your county board of education, get a line on all schools in your community, then have a talk with the director of the school that strikes your fancy.

LANDLORDING. Retired couples are turning out to be fine managers of apartment houses. Not the fancy ones, you understand. The smaller ones. Sometimes there is a free apartment as payment. Sometimes there is small money plus a free apartment. This can be a somewhat rugged job, what with all the complaints of tenants, the collection of rents, and the janitor failing to show up. But it's a job.

GUARDING. Oddly, many jobs for retired people are showing up in the field of security. The warehouse and railroad-crossing watchmen, yes. But many more. Banks and other money institutions are hiring former policemen and retired military personnel as security guards. Large stores, museums, and other places where crowds gather are hiring such people to guide traffic and maintain order. The pay for these jobs is usually the going rate. Employers want the guards for their particular talents and aren't looking for cut-rate deals.

BOOKKEEPING. There are many small businesses, usually on

the outskirts of town, that can and do hire people who know how to keep books and otherwise take care of office details. Such firms seldom need or can afford full-time help, which suits many retired people just fine. The pay would not be large, but the retired person who could handle such a job might well grow into an important job if the business grew, and in any case might well have a job for years.

MOONLIGHTING.   Not in the sense of having two jobs—you'll be happy to get just one—but in the sense of working the hours other people don't like. Say from 4 P.M. to midnight, or midnight to 8 A.M. These jobs are usually found only in the cities, but there are lots of them. You can start with the distributors of morning newspapers and milk, with the garbage collectors, and any of the public utilities. Then check into the all-night restaurants, the maintenance crews of big office buildings. Finally, ask somebody at city hall what businesses operate all night. Or check the firms in the classified section of the phone book and figure it out for yourself.

There are certain avenues to retirement jobs that most people don't explore. The Congressman who represents your district in Washington is always a possibility. And his aim is to please. Sometimes he can't help; sometimes he can. The best approach to him is to write his administrative assistant; any politician in the community will know his name. But I wouldn't bother if I had actively opposed his election in the last campaign.

Your representative in the state legislature may be able to help you. He, like the Congressman, will have no jobs himself. But he may know where some are lurking. Contact him direct. By letter.

A third avenue to a retirement job is the public unemployment office operated usually by the state government in cooperation with the federal government. It often is called the State Employment Office. Usually branches of this office are set up throughout the state, and skilled interviewers try to put you in touch with whatever jobs are available. The jobs as a rule are in the lower categories, but occasionally a good one comes along.

171

Hobbies

There is considerable money to be made out of hobbies if you'll stop treating them as hobbies and get down to business. It is more fun to make retirement money this way than most, since the so-called hobbies are supposed to be a pleasure anyway and you wouldn't be involved in one unless you thought it so.

Walter W. Brackman, a retired industrial foreman, is one of the outstanding examples of a hobbyist-turned-businessman, and this is how he tells the story:

"I had always been something of a nut on tools, mostly woodworking tools," he says. "My wife had allowed me a good corner of the basement for a workshop, and for a good many years I had had a lot of pleasure fixing things and making things.

"As my retirement came on, my wife began secretly saving some dollars out of her budget, and at my retirement party presented me with the most handsome set of wood tools you can imagine. There was a power saw and power drills, with fancy attachments, a small lathe, all sorts of cutting hand tools, a new hammer, and fourteen bags of different-sized nails.

"Well!" What to do with this beautiful loot?

"I spent about a week just admiring it, and testing it. Then I went around the house to re-do professionally some jobs I had earlier done crudely. I made a table and a couple of flower stands for my wife, some more shelves for the basement. Then I had nowhere to go. There's a limit to what you can build for a home."

He says his wife noted his predicament, visualized her fine gift gathering dust, and again acted.

"She apparently wrote letters to half the furniture makers in the country asking for their catalogues. Then she presented them to me and asked why I didn't start making furniture.

"I studied the designs, got a little heated up on the idea of reproducing them. Then I picked a simple dinette set of a table and four chairs, searched around until I found some maple wood, and went to work.

"And I did all right. I ruined a couple of table legs because I was being too fancy, so I changed the design to something I could handle. I made some other changes, too. I finally produced a dinette set about as pretty as any you can find in a store. I knew it. My wife and everybody else who saw it knew it, too.

"So now I took the initiative. I rented a trailer, hooked it onto the back of my car, loaded my dinette set, and started making the rounds of the smaller furniture stores. I told the buyers I could produce sets like this cheaper than anybody, that I would deliver them to the stores unfinished and they could let their customers save money by do-it-yourself varnishing."

Brackman got orders for three dinette sets at the first four stores he visited. He was in business.

"I've been at it nearly six months now, and my problem is whether to stay on with my basement operation and make some nice pocket money or whether to set up an outside shop, hire some help, and make some real money."

W. J. Stoneman preferred fishing to power tools. River fishing mostly, and primarily in Arkansas. He retired and with his wife moved to Arkansas and bought a river farm. A year later, after watching droves of Midwesterners motoring into Arkansas on vacations and needing bait, boats, and fishing tackle, he built a small store on the river just off the highway and set himself up in business as The Trout Terminal. At last reports he was planning to expand by building a row of fisherman's huts with bunks which hard-core fishermen could rent by the day or week to pursue their pleasure along the river.

You can find many people like Brackman and Stoneman who have taken the fiddle-faddle out of a hobby and are making it pay. Miss Cornelia W. Strickman who retired at sixty-two did— with a camera.

"I had been fond of picture-taking for years," she says, "and as time went by I acquired a couple of fine cameras and became fairly expert on the fine points. I got into color, then into slides, and finally into color prints.

"The usual things didn't interest me much, and as I grew older I passed up the children, the dogs, and such subjects and

173

went in for birds and landscapes. I sold a series of my bird pictures to a publisher for inclusion in a bird book. An art gallery took a few of my landscapes, framed them, and sold them for me on a commission basis."

And then she met an imaginative man.

"Why don't we take twelve of the most beautiful landscapes you have and make a calendar?" he asked.

They went to work on the project. They decided to use only landscapes of their state, with winter scenes for the cold months, maple trees for the autumn months, and so forth, and then sell the calendar only in their state. If the project succeeded, they would do the same with adjoining states, and even try a national calendar.

"We took in a third partner," Miss Strickman says. "He was the president of a small printing firm that could reproduce color. Each of us invested $500, and for nearly a year we labored over our calendar design. It couldn't be just another calendar . . . it had to be an art piece."

There was other work—the lining up of retail outlets for the calendar and the soliciting of firms that would make bulk purchases for gifts to their customers. The publisher was the key to this, as in fact he was to the financing of what was a rather expensive idea.

The project panned out. "We are now on our third calendar," Miss Strickman says. "The three partners have long since gotten back their original investment and are making money. And, incidentally, I'm not Miss Strickman anymore. I'm married"—to the imaginative man who got her into all of this.

There are other ways to make money out of a camera hobby. But they had better be off the beaten path. There are too many commercial photographers already, and to turn the hobby into a business of taking pictures of brides and babies doesn't work out too well. You can query a medical school or hospital about taking surgical pictures; book publishers about illustrating some particular type of books; magazine publishers about photographing some particular feature story you have found in your area. The more highly specialized the field, the better you will fare.

You can make extra retirement money by getting into the stamp-collecting and coin-collecting business. But you'll have to be very good and have quite an expensive collection before you can compete with the professionals already at work.

But you can collect glassware, or napkin rings, or hurricane lamps, or antique jewelry, or old crockery, or flatirons, and set up an antique shop in a cubbyhole on a side street. Many women have done this and made money.

Collecting, in the main, is something for your heirs two generations from now to make money on. Just store your treasures away in a trunk and forget them. In fifty years somebody will discover them and make a killing.

There are other hobbies you can convert into money, if you'll keep in mind that the product of the hobby must be something people will pay money for and if you'll capitalize on any local situation that provides a need for your hobby. Suppose, for instance, that you live on a lake or ocean, and you like to play with boats. You can start selling boats, or renting them; open a shop for boat supplies; build a dock and charge landing fees; operate a charter fishing service; set up a repair shop for boat motors.

Or suppose you like to play with toy trains. Set up a repair shop for them in your garage and charge fees; lease a counter in a toy or hobby shop and sell them; start giving exhibitions of your trains, for a fee, at fairs and conventions.

If you write poetry, or think you do, you may make some money selling your output to manufacturers of greeting cards. If you do oil paintings, water colors, etc., make sure you get some fun out of it—you're not going to get much money, ever.

A Personal Business

Setting up a business of your own in retirement is pretty much like turning a hobby into a commercial enterprise. The big difference is that you don't have to like the business.

You can sit back calmly, size up a type of business your community needs, and set out to make some money in it without ever professing it's wonderful. Of course it'll be better to develop some sort of reasonable attachment to the work. It'll go better that way.

Here are some of the personal businesses that have—and haven't—gone well in retirement:

LANDSCAPING. The man or woman with some real knowledge about trees, shrubbery, and flowers can break into the landscaping business with comparative ease. Two keys to success are picking the right community—you don't want an aging one where everything is already planted, but one booming with new subdivisions —and a willingness to try door-to-door selling. A person of retirement age would need young assistants to do the digging and the rough work; would need a contract with a good nursery where plantings of all kinds could be obtained; and would need some kind of headquarters, even if only a shack at the edge of town with a display area, where a garden store could be developed for the motoring shopper.

There are tricks to this trade, as to all of them. A person going into the business for the first time would be wise to get a commission job with some established operator for a few months first and learn the ropes.

BABY-SITTING. This is trivial business if you try it by going around to various clients at so much per hour. But it can be important if you set up a baby-sitter agency and hire others to do the sitting. You need only three tools: a straight-line telephone, a list of dependable sitters, and a modest advertising campaign aimed at prospective clients. The five-hour jobs for parents'-night-out have usually been the basic need of this business, but you would be smart to strike for the bigger deals of supplying house-keepers or foster mothers for a week or so. Husbands travel more than ever now on business trips, and many want their wives along. Young mothers go to hospitals for another baby or an illness and can no longer get their own parents to come in and run the home. An increasing number of husbands and wives like to take flying vacations to Europe without the children. These are the cases that bring the fees which make the business worthwhile.

FARMING. Don't.

SUPPLYING RECREATION.   Retired people who own rural land have been moving in on the recreation business in recent years and doing well at it. Most successful thus far have been those who owned land with a lake on it, or even a large pond. They have stocked their water with fish and charged so much per hour, or so much per pound caught, as the city dwellers come out to cast.

Some people have turned their farmlands into hunting preserves, again charging a fee for hunting. Others owning land along a picturesque river or in the mountains are building cabins which they rent to weekenders or vacationists.

(All these things of course have their fringe benefits—the snack stand, sports shop, grocery shop, etc.—which also produce income.)

OPERATING A TRAILER PARK.   This is a rapidly growing business, and retired people are good at it. By the thousands, travelers are crisscrossing the country in every form of trailer or mobile home. Parking places for overnight or a week are not plentiful. The business is not complicated, but you'll need some expert advice. You can get it from the Mobile Homes Manufacturers Association, 20 North Wacker Drive, Chicago, Illinois 60606.

TREE-CUTTING.   This, oddly, is a pretty good small business. But you have to know what you're doing. And you've got to pick the right community—in brief, one that has a lot of residential trees in it. You'll need some strong labor to do the work—you have no business climbing trees after sixty-five—a truck to haul away the debris, and some power saws. There's a simple way to get your business: you just ride through the residential areas and spot the dead trees. Then ring the doorbell.

DRESSMAKING.   This is one of the ancient occupations of women. It is still in demand. Not so much for making frocks, but for remodeling them, along with children's clothes, men's trousers, and such. Many modern women can't sew, don't even have sewing machines, and are throwing away a lot of money in clothes that could be salvaged.

RUNNING A HAMBURGER SHOP.   Forget it. Too many chain operators are taking over the business.

BEING A MR. FIX-IT.   This is a retirement business a man and his wife can operate. The modern home has become a palace of appliances, all of which break down. And what happens? The housewife calls somebody to come fix what has just broken down —the furnace, air conditioner, refrigerator, toilet, lights in the kitchen, stove, TV set, radio, electric clock, vacuum cleaner, something. The somebody she calls says, well, maybe they can be out tomorrow to fix it. When tomorrow? Well, maybe tomorrow morning.

So the housewife postpones all her errands, stays home, and somebody doesn't show up. So in the late afternoon she goes out to do her errands. And somebody shows up. He finds nobody home, goes away. About three days of this sort of thing and the housewife and fixer finally get together. But then the fixer has to take some major segment of the gadget away so he can order a special part from Pittsburgh. Which will be here next Thursday. So she stays home Thursday, all day. It comes Friday.

This sort of business is driving America's modern housewives batty. They are living in a mechanical, electrical, and electronic world, don't know how to keep this sort of world in repair, and are at the mercy of service men who can't, or won't give them the service they need at the time they need it, or are promised it.

The average retired man who has lived in a home for many years knows how to fix most stubborn appliances. At least he knows where to go to get them fixed. He can set himself up as a Mr. Fix-it, let housewives know he can solve their problems with the gadgets, and make a reputation and some money. But he needs his wife in the business with him—to make him go to a lady's house to fix something when he said he would. Men just don't understand.

Now, In Addition . . .

The size of the pension you have when you go into retirement will most likely remain static from now on. This is not because the company is a skinflint, as some suppose. It is because the number of dollars in the pension is all you and the company have bought and paid for. Through your working years you and the company, or just the company, agreed to contribute so many dollars per month to the pension. The books on this agreement close at retirement time, and the dollars accumulated are used to pay the best pension available. No more dollars, no bigger pension. So don't expect to increase your retirement income from this source.

The size of your Social Security will probably go slowly upward as long as you live. Congress decides this, on the basis of rising living costs, new Social Security taxes, and the general status of the Social Security fund. So by voting for the right Congressman you may bolster your chances to increase your income from this source.

You can increase your retirement income by trading in the stock market. But you'll have to be smart, and you'll need a wide knowledge of stock-market operation. Otherwise you'll lose your candy. Oddly, a large number of retired men with small resources play a cat-and-mouse game with the market and can pick up a few dollars a day from it. You can see them in the board rooms of stockbrokers in most major cities. They drift in during the morning, take a back seat, and watch the trading. Then they walk over and buy a couple of shares of some stock they think will be rising during the day. It rises. They sell, pocket their profit after paying their commissions, and come back tomorrow to try again. If they are astute enough, they average out pretty well, and they have themselves an absorbing time while doing it. It is not recommended—repeat *not*—that you engage in this sort of game to increase your retirement income. But if you have a couple of hundred dollars you can play with, know what you are doing, and find hanging around a board room more interesting than hanging around the living room, you might have a look.

And, finally, one last way to increase your income. It has been held until last because it fits no one category that has gone before, but virtually all of them. And because it may prove the most satisfying of all to you:

You come up to retirement belonging to something. You really wouldn't be an American—or you'd be ill—if you didn't. You belong to the Lions Club, Kiwanis, or Civitan, to a fraternity, to a secret order, to a labor union, to an alumni association, to the chamber of commerce, to a church—certainly to something. Well, virtually all such organizations have headquarters and paying jobs and a big heart for a brother or sister who has been paying dues.

Look into the regional or national headquarters setup of whatever you belong to, get a recommendation from your local chieftain, then go offer your wholehearted services to this splendid organization. For a salary.

You see, you aren't really asking for a job. You just want to contribute your talents to the fine work the organization is doing on a larger scale than heretofore. And you would accept a salary to offset your added expenses, etc. All members of all organizations naturally can't land jobs in the regional or national headquarters. But many are doing it. And image-wise, among their friends, they are walking tall because they aren't working again to make money—they are working to further the good works of a good organization.

TWELVE

⌒

THE WOMAN OR MAN WHO RETIRES ALONE

This is the retirement story of the single woman, the single man, the widow, and the widower. Of these, the most restless is the widower.

But the single woman upstages him. She is the most prominent loner now retiring, and in many ways the most significant. She is the newest of the lot, for one thing, because it has been only in recent years that the uninhibited career woman has come upon the scene to work alongside the man and to win the right to whatever rewards he gets upon retirement.

Except for some schoolteachers and government employees, the retired single woman on a pension is still somewhat a novelty. But she won't be for long because a veritable army of them went to work in World War II, stayed, and are now in shouting distance of a pension.

So they take precedence.

The Single Woman

If you are one these, and if there's a pension in your future, the first thing to do—and right away—is to admit how old you are.

It'll hurt only a little. And won't be fatal.

You're going to have to do this sooner or later. You'll have to give proof of birth to get your Social Security and probably to get your pension. Then there's the matter of your life insurance. Retirement for the single woman has become the moment of truth on age.

Of course, *you* may have been telling the truth about your age since you passed twenty-six. In which case just pass this on to any twenty other single women you know, who probably haven't.

In coming up to your confession of age, if you've been cheating a bit on the business and government forms you've signed, the wisest thing to do is to go see the personnel officer, to blush a little, to smile, and to tell him the truth. The personnel officer of a good company or institution, in these days, is a man of heart. He has to be. Or he wouldn't have that fine desk and title. And he understands many things, among them the sad fact that women do—and have to—lie about their age. Yours will not be the first confession he has heard.

The personnel officer can tell you how to get out of your dilemma provided you are honest with him. Which means you had better not tell him you really don't know your age because the courthouse where your birth records were kept burned down.

He will tell you various ways to get acceptable proof of your right age, if you actually don't know it. He may tell you, but with kindness, that however much he may sympathize with what you have done, the concealment of your age in modern times can create serious complications. Which it can. In addition to jeopardizing your retirement benefits to a fare-thee-well, it can defer or advance your retirement date.

The personnel officer will not print in the employee magazine your confession of age. He will keep your secret. So go on and see him.

Once you've done this—and you're going to have a number of sessions with this man before things are straightened out, not just one—you will know him well enough to discuss another matter of age with him. Ask him what would be the results of your retiring a bit early.

182

If you can retire early, it may be an advantage to you for the next twenty years, particularly if you are sensitive about your age, which you should be. The reason it is an advantage is fairly obvious. Most people you know are aware of the retirement age for women at your company—age sixty, sixty-two, or sixty-five. So, if you retire normally you are naturally that old. But if you retire even six months early, and word goes out that you are giving up your job before retirement date, then you and the beauty shop can keep you forty-nine years old from here on.

"But," as one such woman has said, "you've got to be able to grab your mail out of the box before anybody sees it. Because once they see a Social Security envelope addressed to you, they'll know for sure that you're at least sixty-two. . . . And by the way, why can't Social Security mail women their checks in plain envelopes?"

Here is a breakdown for the life of the single woman going into retirement:

RESIDENCE.   In general, a city is the best place of residence for the single woman. It has more of the things that can make life good for you after age sixty—entertainment, museums, libraries, schools, clubs. A small town would be more friendly. In fact a city can be very lonely for the single woman. But you are conditioned for loneliness. All your years of single life have taught you how to stand alone. Of all people coming up to retirement age you are the best equipped mentally to be lonely. You are best supplied with possible companions because most cities and towns are dotted with other older women who are alone.

HOUSING.   The single woman in retirement seems inclined to live in an apartment, which is about the loneliest place in a city to live. But it has great virtues of safety and convenience. You should at least look into the possibility of acquiring a house that contains an apartment and bringing a young couple with a baby or two to live in it. Some retired single women have found a completely new world in becoming involved in the lives of such a young family. Others have found deep satisfaction in the social intercourse that a house, but not an apartment, can bring from neighbors.

SOCIAL LIFE.   There is practically none of it, in the normal sense, for the single retired woman. Social habits of the day—dinner parties, dances, cocktail parties—just do not have a natural place for you. For several reasons, but primarily because there is a great scarcity of single men your age to pair off with you. Your social activities must be centered in the clubs and organizations you join, and in whatever social affairs they arrange as an adjunct to their primary missions in life. For instance, the D.A.R. wouldn't be throwing many gay parties on a Friday night, but the Society for Crippled Children or the Rheumatism Foundation might.

So choose carefully the organizations you will join, checking them out first in the society columns of the newspaper to see whether they just read the minutes of the last meeting or have some fun. It is really not difficult to join just about any organization that strikes your fancy. You can't get into the Georgia Chapter of the United Daughters of the Confederacy if your grandpa marched to the sea with Sherman. But you can get into most organizations because most of them are constantly seeking members and workers.

TRAVEL.   Don't, for goodness' sake, do what the average single retired woman has been doing for the last fifteen years: which has been to go on a cruise on a freighter, join a guided tour of Europe, go to resorts where all the other single women go. Most of you have been looking a little silly on your travels, and don't have to. Because whether you have been looking for companionship, marriage, or pleasure, you can do better.

The freighter cruise is all right, if you want a slow, quiet voyage on which you will meet very few people and have very little excitement. Boredom is the order of the day. So is it on the luxury ocean liners, except there you can be caught up in a steady social program carefully designed to mix you with other people and give you enjoyment.

The guided tour is safe and protects you from the embarrassments of not knowing the mechanics of travel. But other travelers looking for this safety and protection are not always the most exciting traveling companions. And you should be aware that the little clusters of travelers on guided tours look a bit forlorn as they stand around airports and hotel lobbies waiting for laggards. They are frequently the butt of ridicule by more sophisticated travelers.

As for the resorts, well, there's just no point to a camp-out with the same sex and age—at least for a woman. Men, even if you don't want any of them, and varying age groups, even if they annoy you, make for more magic at a resort. It has often seemed that older single women all get the same travel brochures and all wind up at the same resorts at the same time.

So, on travel, determine first that you will seek something all the other single women aren't going for. Then determine, if at all possible, not to go with another single woman your age. Your chances of getting to know men on your travels, and your chances of any special activities with new people you meet—men, women, or youngsters—are greatly hampered when there are two of you instead of one. You can travel with an older aunt or uncle, or with a young nephew or niece, and a new friend you meet would not mind asking you to leave your companion behind and come along. But when your companion is a woman your age—no. A new friend is obligated to ask you both, or go off to a bar. He'll usually choose the bar.

Where to go? It doesn't really matter since everybody is going everywhere now, so long as you are *sure* it is not an "Old Maid Trip." Any travel agent, any airline, and some resorts will guide you right if you are bold enough to say you don't want an "Old Maid Trip," which, from almost everybody, is what you'll get if you aren't bold enough.

You can travel alone in safety to just about any spot in the United States and to the major cities of Canada and Western Europe. Single women are doing it all the time. Airlines in particular will see that you have no embarrassment if you haven't traveled much. The good resorts and ship lines are careful about this, too. Lasting friends by the thousands are now being made by people on long airline trips, particularly to Europe and particularly in the economy compartments. Lasting friends are being made by Americans on ships, but to Europe and Asia more than to the island resorts. And usually more in first class than second. They are being made from Westminster to the Louvre to St. Peter's and other such gathering points of American travelers in Europe. They are being made at resorts from Maine to Mexico so long as the resorts have a mixture of guest—not just women, not just old folks, not just teen-agers.

Travel by car, while best for some retired people, is usually not best for the single woman alone. There's less safety. There's less opportunity for her to meet other people and go after things that are enjoyable.

MARRIAGE.   It is now generally recognized that many women who come up to retirement as single women have had marriage proposals, have turned them down, and in fact have never wanted to marry. Be that as it may, the richest life a single woman can find at retirement is marriage. To a decent man, naturally. Not to an adventurer or a social bankrupt.

There are some deep personal problems in marriage for a woman of this age. Sex is one. But a woman marrying a man in his sixties can probably take it or leave it. In any case she is old enough to discuss the matter with the man and have an understanding before marriage. In the main, the single woman past sixty marrying a man of that age would not have to contend with sex.

A second problem to a woman is money. If she is sacrificing any part of her financial security in order to marry—she is too old ever to regain it herself—then the man she marries must provide that she will have security in case of a divorce or his death.

A third problem is the children of the man she marries, because it is usually only widowers who marry after age sixty. These children can be suspicious of the woman's intentions from the start, can make marriage miserable for her. She must demand from the man that he establish some sort of basis of understanding between herself and these children, and that he give them assurance that she is not coming into his life to snatch his money or to smear the memory of their mother.

With these matters solved, if they can be, a single retired woman can discover a magnificent world of affection, companionship, and emotional security in marriage. And all sorts of doors to life's enjoyments that are closed to her would open.

So, if she chooses to marry, where is the right man? He could well be sitting in the living room of what has been his family home, smoking too much and drinking too much, wondering what he's going to do tomorrow or next week, trying to figure which restaurant to go to for dinner tonight, how he's going to get a maid to keep the house in order, and whether he should move into a hotel. He would be a widower, a fairly recent one, and he would be a lost soul.

You might try selling encyclopedias door-to-door and discover such an eligible widower. It would be a long chance. Better that you should try to determine where a widower would go and how you could meet him under proper circumstances. The atmosphere is too thick at the time of the funeral of a man's wife for him to have any thoughts of a remarriage. But there have been a number of women involved in such funerals, with a funeral home, florist shop, cemetery, etc., who have developed an acquaintanceship made with the widower there into a friendship and marriage. Women who have been involved in the cleanup of such a funeral—lawyer's assistants, insurance people, friends of the late wife who later came in to assort, pack, or distribute her personal things—have developed friendships with widowers into marriage.

Beyond the sadness period, a woman should figure where a widower might go to fill the emptiness of life that has come upon him. To his private club, for sure, if he has one. To meetings of all the organizations he belongs to, from his church to the American Legion. And into any kinds of sports, but particularly golf and fishing.

You can do some of your traveling to the resorts that specialize in golf, fishing, and hunting. You can keep your eye watchful at church. You can look into membership in any man-woman organization that has older members. You can be nicer than usual to any busy hostess you know, because after six months or so she will start inviting any widower she knows to all kinds of parties, what with the scarcity of unattached men.

Above all you should keep in mind what this widower wants, not what you want. He wants, basically, to have another woman around who will take care of him. Not a sleek female, not a bedroom friend, not a glamour girl, not even a pretty one. He wants a comfortable one and, almost without exception, a good one.

You will note that everything said until now concerns widowers, with no mention of older bachelors. Older bachelors are hardly worth mentioning where marriage is involved.

You should understand that you can buy a husband. Many are for sale. Some of them are very pretty. In almost any fashionable resort area you can see older women with younger playboys at their elbows. The price of husbands on this level is high. But the price and the prettiness of husbands drop from this level all the way down to the cheap retirement hotels where older men struggling along on Social Security will be very happy to marry any woman who can add some extra change to the cookie jar.

You should understand also—and understand this well—that some single women of retirement age decide they have to prove a point on marriage. They *can* marry, if they want to. So they show their friends by going out and picking up some degenerate, so long as he's wearing shoes and a tie. They are as foolish as, if not more foolish than, the retired single woman who falls for the lover bit from a man who romances her—at her age— because of the wonder of her deep gray eyes . . . and who is after something.

For the notebook of the single woman:
You need a lawyer for a confidential friend, much more than most retired people. You don't have the close kin or usually the reliable friends who can step in at times of crisis to help you, or to handle your affairs properly when you die. So make a friend of a lawyer—a widower, maybe.

A curse that hangs over your head, if you are a single woman, is that you are prim. It is probably a legitimate curse because most women who reach the sixties without marrying actually *are* prim in their behavior, their dress, and their conversation. In an age of four-letter words and double-bed novels it doesn't quite fit. Don't go out and start cussing, but you might read a few of the modern novels and buy yourself some come-on clothes.

Consider setting aside as much as $500 (if you have some savings) for the specific purpose of improving the way you look. Go to a fine beauty shop—not the one in the shopping center, now—and pay whatever the cost to have a professional decide the most attractive hairdo and makeup you can have. Take the advice you get. Then go to the effort and small expense of subscribing to at least two fashion magazines, and after you've read them for a couple of months, go buy some clothes that enhance your image. To a fashionable store, not to the racks in somebody's budget basement. If you have not had the personal attention in your life that you might deserve, it could well be because of the way you look. It's worth $500 to find out, if you've got $500.

If you haven't, you may be able to get it out of your life insurance. What have you got life insurance for, anyway? You have no dependents to suffer if you die. And the notion many older single women get about leaving money to nieces and nephews is so much nonsense. Huge amounts of life insurance have been sold to single women. They go into their retirement with it. What do they need it for, beyond the expenses of a reasonable funeral? And should a retired single woman be more concerned about leaving money to unappreciative cousins than to enhancing her own life?

As you are debating these suggestions, start going to church regularly. You are not likely to make many friends there. In fact you may sit in your pew for a year and get nothing but a few polite bows from the pastor and his flock. But volunteer to join whatever good works the church is doing. If you will work a little harder than others, which will hardly strain you, you will in time take over some office and gain a position of some importance in the congregation. And make some friends. But you'll get nowhere, except maybe to Heaven, if you go and just sit. You'll have to work at it.

You may want to consider a retirement job. You can make friends and develop a social life with a job. But normally you will get a job only below the status level of the career you've had, which means the friends and social affairs will also be below your status level.

You might try going to night school. Every city has such schools for adults now. They are informal, friendly, and frequently interesting. But don't go to a class that's studying lampshades. Pick one where men as well as women are studying.

The Single Man

If you are a man who has come up to age sixty-five without marrying, you don't need this book. The odds are that you won't read it if it's handed to you.

You have learned to keep your house, obtain your own food, and content yourself without the services or the charms of a woman. Retirement for you will be no problem. It will bring no material change in your way of doing things. Just more time to do them.

Marriage is a better life than bachelorhood. But if you've avoided it this long, you're not about to take any advice here that you go get a wife. You probably would have a difficult time adjusting to marriage now anyway.

Your retirement years would be happier if you had some young people around who cared for you. You might consider taking under your wing a nephew you like and see him through his education and into a career, or a young married couple related to you that is struggling through the economics of establishing their first home. Attention and help from you could endear such younger relatives to you and could bring you some deep satisfactions that a bachelor usually does not get.

You probably have some money stored away. A bachelor by age sixty-five usually does. Has anybody told you you can't take it with you? If you are a fisherman, you might like to try a little casting in some of the South American rivers. And there's some good hunting in Canada. The pyramid country of Egypt, the Holy Land, Venice, the art treasures of Europe—these, they say, are quite a sight to see.

The Widow

The widow who retires alone, in what follows here, will be the bereaved or divorced woman who works, and the wife of the working man, who by retirement time must start thinking of the day she may become a widow.

The working widow goes into retirement with many of the same problems and advantages the single woman has. But there are differences. The widow is usually not so sensitive about her age, is slightly more desirable socially, and less inhibited about life in general.

Some widows have a siren complex at retirement time, but it takes some paint and pretending to put it across after age sixty. Some have a strong yen to remarry, and since they have more sophistication—and there is always a certain magic about widows —they can usually do it with more ease than the single woman.

But the greatest difference between the widow and single woman is family. The widow frequently has children. And for good or ill, they exercise strong influence on the way she retires.

If you are a widow who is retiring between sixty and sixty-five, your children would probably be in their forties, well established in their mode of life, and getting along. They don't need you, but if they have affection for you, they would like you within reach, and on occasion could use you to take over their household and baby-sit for their own children. You probably don't need them, but you love them and could use them as well as problems come on in later years.

You might consider choosing your retirement home in a locality where one of your married children lives. Not in the same house, not next door. Maybe around the corner or down the street. You might give serious thought to living in a house instead of an apartment so other children and grandchildren living out of town could come visiting.

But if you move near your children, or acquire a home large enough to supply them free visits, be careful that you do not subjugate your own life to theirs. Remain a person in your own right, no matter what. You will presumably have a pension and Social Security and thus will have financial independence. You also have, as a working widow, the self-reliance to stand alone. A woman who has been out in the world working until retirement time doesn't need anybody to hold her hand. And she makes a mistake that can pain her all the way to the grave when she goes to her children in search of comforting arms.

A great advantage the working widow has as she approaches retirement—and among women it is almost exclusive with her—is that she knows something about money. She has been earning so much per week, collecting it, spending it, saving it. The single woman, of course, has been doing the same. But the widow has in her background a family or at least a husband and has been involved with money on a much broader scale.

It is rather difficult for a man to marry a working woman for her money. Or to romance her out of it. Or to sell her an oil well. This is not so true of the retired single woman or the nonworking wife who has been left a widow.

Any working widow will run up against some problems after she retires, even if she has sufficient income for her needs or doesn't buy an oil well. Loneliness will be one of these problems because friends still working at the company will begin drifting away, and other retired friends frequently live too far away for practical visiting. Leisure will be another because a woman who has gone through the care and feeding of a husband, the rearing of babies, and finally the responsibility of a regular job does not find it easy to sit down and knit. Nor do housework and cooking have their old appeal.

When the working widow finds these problems difficult to solve, she might well look into the possibility of a retirement job. Not so much for the extra money but for the worthwhile filling of her idle hours and for the cultivation of new friends. Few things offer the older widow a better chance for friendship than a job, even if it's selling notions behind a dime-store counter. And the working widow, having fewer inhibitions than the single woman, can often capitalize on her working talents to get one.

Here are two working widows, both motivated by a need to keep active and a desire for more friends, who got retirement jobs at opposite ends of the spectrum:

Mrs. Walter J. Spearman, an office employee with a corporation: "I had been with my company for twenty-six years, doing shorthand and typing and general office chores. When the revolution in office machines got under way, my company joined it and began bringing in monsters and gadgets nobody had ever seen before. I was intrigued. I asked and got permission to take special training courses in operation of the machines, which put me one up on most of the women in the office. In the two years before I retired I was virtually in charge of the computers and other sophisticated machines that were constantly coming in.

"So when I retired I knew I had a special knowledge to sell. And I really didn't want to sit home fondling a cat. I wrote three manufacturers of modern office machines, told them I wanted to apply my knowledge of their products by teaching others how to operate them, and asked if they could tell me of any large organizations in my area that were about to convert over to computer office systems.

"You see, I was offering them an advantage as well as seeking one for myself. They would be pleased indeed if an expert were handy to teach people how to operate their machines.

"I got two very pleasant responses from my letters. One offered me a job with the manufacturer, to serve as a trainer on its sales staff. But the other told me that four of the major departments in my state government were now buying computers and apparently had nobody who knew how to operate them.

"There was a bit of commotion after this. Trips to the state capital, conferences with department heads, reference checks with my old company, and finally a visit from the state legislator of my district. It suffices to say that I am now employed at a good salary by the state, work thirty-five hours a week, travel widely over the state on expense accounts teaching employees how to handle their new machines, and am finding politicians and political appointees a strange but fascinating group of animals."

Mrs. Spearman retains her company pension while she works

at her new job. She is deferring her Social Security benefits because she is making more than five times as much money as the limit she would be allowed to make and collect the benefits. In due time, when she gives up her training job, she will make application for Social Security.

Mrs. James J. Horner took the low road instead of the high one, and in several ways has picked more fruit than Mrs. Spearman: "The work I had done with my company had no special application to any retirement job. I really had nothing to sell but myself.

"But I had read the newspapers enough, and watched the executives in my company enough, to know that there was an acute need for substitute mothers in the homes in all fine residential areas. The servant class is virtually gone. The 'domestic class,' as we call it now, is not satisfactory. And these developments have come at a time when the more privileged married couples want to take pleasure junkets as never before, when business executives are traveling all over the earth, wanting to take their wives with them, and when nice homes to be cared for and children to be tended are fouling up the works.

"I visited one of the top employment agencies in town, explained I had reared three children of my own, had been a working widow, had reasonable manners and some knowledge of the world, and could supply references on my character, personality, and temper. I said I wanted work as a substitute mother, for a minimum of a week at a time, in a home where the father and mother wanted to take a trip alone.

"I then wrote letters, saying about the same, to three of the top private clubs in town, including two country clubs. I sent the letters to the club secretaries. I also wrote similar letters to the presidents of three of the leading women's organizations in town."

It was about two weeks before she had her first response— from one of the private clubs. It was to ask her to take over management of a nice home with three children for a week while the parents went to New York. This job led to two others from friends of the parents. Then came calls from women in the organizations.

"For a year I made some substantial money. I had some delightful adventures. . . . And I got a lot of indignant back-talk from my children who were embarrassed, they said, that I was doing this kind of work. So at the end of a year I quit taking private cases—I took a permanent one. With a wealthy family, with luxurious home and grounds, four children, and busy lives that took the parents away from home about half the time. I have a title as 'Home Manager' and live in a private apartment on the grounds. I get fringe benefits labor unions never heard of, such as trips with the family to places like Phoenix and Palm Beach about twice a year. I get vacations, days off, and good pay."

The Widowed Housewife

The wife of a man now working and nearing retirement need not concern herself with morbid thoughts of widowhood. But she would be wise at this point in her married life to consider the possibility that she may eventually be a widow, and take certain precautionary steps. She can come upon disaster if she doesn't.

Wives who become widows after their husbands retire are usually inclined to retire from an active role in life. Friends have been primarily other couples she and her husband knew. They drift away after a while. Outside activity has usually been in companionship with her husband, and when she is left a widow, she does not have the experience of being out alone in the world that the working widow has, and frequently clings close to the security of her home. Her children become the primary interest of her life.

To get on top of this kind of situation—to have in widowhood a life that is not resignation but which has purpose and interest —a wife might take note of the following:

1. Urge your husband to tell you all there is to know about any savings the two of you have—where they are kept, why they are there instead of somewhere else, and what interest they pay.

2. Have him tell you—and write it down—whether his pension will pay you in case he dies and how much, what your Social Security will be, and whether any health insurance he has will continue in force for you.

3. Have him tell you where he keeps all valuable papers of the family, such as deeds, contracts, wills, life insurance policies.

4. Make a careful appraisal of your home, if you own it and plan to live in it in retirement, to make sure it is not so run down that you would have difficulty maintaining it if you were left alone. If it is, consider using savings to put it in order while your husband is around to supervise, or consider moving into a small new house that will require no upkeep.

5. Give long consideration to any plans your husband may have for moving to another town in retirement. Would it be a town where you would want to live as a widow, if you ever had to?

6. Have your husband work out for you, on paper, three columns of figures showing (a) what your monthly income will be from pension, Social Security, annuities, etc., (b) what income there will be from savings and investments and the dates on which this income is paid, and (c) the total amount of money in savings and investments. Have him include in these figures any money you will get from his life insurance, and you might ask him how he has arranged for this insurance to be paid to you. As a monthly income? If in a lump sum how does he think you should invest it?

7. You are beginning to push things by now, but if you think he can stand a bit more, ask him to write down for you when and where you can apply for your increased Social Security benefits if he should die; how you apply for his Social Security death benefit; what officer at your company she should contact if there are any questions concerning your pension or insurance there; how to contact his life insurance company; what to do with his will.

Your husband can pass along this vital information to you in one unpleasant evening. Insist that he do it. Then the both of you get the whole business off your minds.

Women who retire alone, except perhaps the working widow, are candidates for retirement homes sooner than most other retired people. They see them as havens of safety and security, as the most reliable places to take care of them if infirmities come. Their reasoning is good. But they don't have to be in the hurry that some women are. If their health is reasonably good, they might wait until about age seventy, and then start looking into the possibility of reserving space in a retirement home for the day when they'll need it. A home operated without profit by a religious, fraternal, or labor union if possible, rather than a privately operated home, is best.

The Widower

After years of studying the plight of the retired widower, appraising his peculiar problems, his sensibilities, his charm, his frailties, his miseries, the exclusiveness of his role in society, the wide demand for his company, and the fact that he is house-broken, the author has come to the conclusion that the best advice that can be given to him is:

"Go get married!"

Widowers, except for those who have been widowers for a long time and have adjusted, are the lost souls of retirement. They don't know how to live without a companion to talk to. They don't like anything about the situation. If they have had a wife to take their pulse all these years, to feed them, listen to them, make their beds, and keep their nest habitable, they simply don't know how to manage alone.

Widowers are in great demand as husbands. Even sorry ones. A widower need only to watch the verandas of retirement hotels in sunshine country, the lobbies of the better residential hotels in the cities, the front pews of his church, the membership roster of any women's organization in town, and he will be struck by the great preponderance of widows over widowers. Many of them are charming. Some are rich. Not all of them of course want to remarry, but a proper widower could close his eyes and throw a dart and probably hit one who does.

One word of caution if you are a widower: Don't marry if you are looking only for a housekeeper, a cook, a servant, or somebody to keep the dust wiped from the photograph of your former wife. Plan to honor her as a wife and respect her, and be kind—or prepare for an education in misery, the like of which you never dreamed of.

THIRTEEN

CONQUERING YOUR WORRIES
ABOUT RETIREMENT

You will be getting no Points A, B, and C in this chapter. The lessons have gone before, and it is time now to ease into a comfortable chair and do a bit of reflecting.

Just what is retirement? With the money, the doctors, the lawyers, the where-to-move, and such out of the way, what does retirement in our time boil down to? What is its significance to you as a lone human being?

You might reflect first on the idea that, as you reach retirement, you have company. There are something like 20 million retired people in the country now, and on the day you reach age sixty-five about 3,700 other Americans are doing the same. That's 3,700 a *day*. You'll have company all right.

But you have more than that. You have two other generations of people walking along with you through the retirement process, a fact that is not yet appreciated or fully understood. When you retire, say at sixty-five, your grandchildren are about at the age to enter the business world. Somebody's grandchild will get a job because you are retiring. And might not otherwise. Business has to work on a budget of people as well as of money. It has figured, for example, that it can afford two hundred people for certain of its operations. That is all. Since it is reluctant to fire people or lay them off, its best opportunity in hiring young people is frequently when its older people retire. In fact, it can sometimes afford to hire two young people for the salary it was paying a sixty-five-year-old employee. Some business firms now plot their hiring of the young on the age scale of their older employees. Next year it can hire ten, the year after fifteen, and so on.

Grandchildren don't yet realize that they are often getting their first break on a job because Grandpa or Grandma retired.

Your own children, as well as your grandchildren, are going through the retirement process with you. They are a bit more aware of it than your grandchildren, but even they don't fully appreciate it yet. Your children, as you reach sixty-five, are usually in their forties. These are the most expensive years of their family lives, the most intense years of their business lives. Their own children are in the college years. The family status as measured by a nice home and a new car is on the line. And health problems of Mother and Dad begin to show up. Money, in the forties, is paramount. And this in turn makes the business career paramount—a better job, more money.

Your retirement has two vital effects on this situation. You give up your job and take your pension, and the son of somebody your age can move up to your job and your salary. And if you are with a good company and getting a good pension, you move out into retirement without having to call on your children for financial help at this most expensive time of their lives. Men and women who work for good companies and are now retiring— you, for instance—are a new breed in mankind's history. Never before have older people been able to give up their working careers without calling on their children for help.

The in-between ages go through the retirement process with you, too. The married couples in their early thirties, with babies, 2 A.M. feedings, mortgages, hurly-burly, time payments, and diapers, long mightily for the peace and freedom of retirement. Don't scoff at this—it's true. The most appealing letters the author of these words has had over the last twenty years have come from young mothers asking what kind of insurance they can buy for a secure retirement and an early one.

Then there are those in their fifties. People usually discover retirement about age fifty-five with a "Gee, it's a-coming!" They start hurrying to pay off their mortgage and store some nuts. And conniving on ways to beat it or capitalize on it. And reading the fine print on their insurance policies for the first time. And making guarded inquiries about this funny thing the company has called a "retirement plan."

So retirement is not a copyrighted thing which you and others in their sixties own. It extends across the age spectrum from twenty-one to sixty-five.

You understand, of course, that in conquering any worry you may have about retirement you will conquer it through your own mental processes. Not through any words of cheer given you here, or anywhere else. Not through any rah-rah nonsense about "how *wonderful* everything's going to be for you!"

Retirement is *not* altogether wonderful. It has problems. It takes some thinking and it takes some planning. It is, in fact, one of the most dramatic events of your life. But there are ways to handle it, and once you handle it you are off on what is, without question, the greatest and most meaningful adventure of your life.

You need some facts and you need, indeed, some perspective which these words and those you get from your employer can give you. Take them at their face value, and as you sit back in your easy chair, reflect on them. If you do, whatever worries you have will pass.

You should reflect very long and hard on just what sort of human package you are—you who at this point in the twentieth century are coming up for retirement. You are probably ornery some of the time, have bunions, some varicose veins, won't comb your hair, and haven't contributed as much to the church as you should. But you who are coming up to retirement in this particular age are probably the most remarkable human beings history has seen.

You were born in the early 1900's. And in a world that has often gone crazy over the last sixty years and that still caters to the survival of the fittest, you have survived.

You survived the baby diseases that were still rampant then.

You survived the carnage of World War I. You survived the flu epidemic that followed it. You didn't poison yourself on the home brew and the bathtub gin of the 1920's. You survived the Depression—many families didn't. You survived Hitler, Mussolini, Franco, World War II, and Korea. As of today you have survived cancer, heart attacks, Communists, jealous lovers, automobiles, and teen-agers.

Think of the millions of people in your generation who didn't survive these things. The mere fact that you are alive and able to be reading these words now is substantial evidence that you have had a charmed life, or that you are an extraordinary human package.

You can nurse a worry over surviving retirement. It's free. Nobody will stop you. But if any man or woman in all history has had reason for faith in surviving it, you are it.

If you can master your worries about survival—and again it's up to you to put two and two together and figure it out for yourself—you next should devote a few minutes of thinking to your abilities to adjust to the changes of retirement. You have learned to adjust about as well as you have learned to survive in your sixty-odd years.

You adjusted, in the Depression, from a prosperous life to government handouts, eviction from your apartment, cancellation of your telephone service, threats of legal suits by your creditors, foreclosures on any mortgage you had signed, a cut in pay, and/or loss of your job. Well, maybe *you* didn't. But three other guys living on your street did. At least you saw the breadlines and what was happening.

And you were no kid in the early thirties. You were old enough to understand and suffer at least a little. You adjusted to this catastrophe.

You adjusted and kept your balance when the wave of "isms," including communism and socialism, swept over the country in the wake of the Depression. You adjusted to the concepts of the Roosevelt New Deal, which in their day were pretty bizarre to most people: TVA, NRA, PWA, packing of the Supreme Court, third term and fourth term, and that queer business called Social

Security which you'd have to pay into for some thirty years before you could collect.

You adjusted to World War II, but we've always adjusted to wars pretty well. You adjusted to what seemed frightful income taxes. To a transition from a horse and buggy which you started life in to jet airplanes. To the vast growth of labor unions and a gigantic uplift of "the common man." To the idea of paid-up pensions and health insurance. And over the last few years to the profound thing called civil rights.

Do you know what was perhaps your greatest mental adjustment? If you were a normal youngster in a God-fearing home on a farm or in a small town, as you probably were, it was very likely the Scopes Monkey Trial in Tennessee. Remember? It was when Clarence Darrow, the famed lawyer, shook the foundations of faith a nation had always lived by.

You've adjusted . . . all your life and to bizarre developments. Right now you are adjusting to the proposition that not Heaven but Outer Space is Way Up Yonder.

So you'll have trouble adjusting to retirement? Not if you'll reflect a bit.

The fact that millions of other people are walking with you through the retirement process should give you some courage for your future. The fact that your record for physical survival and for adjustment is unique should give you some faith. There is one other matter about you as a person that you might take a hardheaded look at.

As you come up to retirement, you are painted in the public's image somewhat as old-fashioned. There's nothing new in this; people in their sixties or so have always been painted as old-fashioned. But in modern times the brush seems to have gotten bigger, and the paint more vivid. You are about the most old-fashioned person who ever reached the sixties, what with space, electronics, and computers.

You have no Ph.D. degrees from a university in these things. You're just not with it because you're so old. And as you hear this kind of talk, you may feel inclined to put on a sackcloth coat and creep into retirement with a bowed head and a large-sized inferiority complex.

The whole thing is silly. And one wonders who is propagandizing the libel. The young, maybe? Who would like to discredit you out of the picture sooner and get your job?

In your lifetime you have seen the infernal gasoline machine come on the scene to replace the deliveryman with horse and dray, the blacksmith, the mule trader, the buggy salesman. Electricity replace the oil lamp. Television and radio replace the Gramophone. Freezers replace iceboxes. Gas replace stovewood. Nylon replace silk. Air conditioning replace pasteboard fans.

You have lived through all these without becoming old-fashioned. And they weren't Bush League technological changes. They were profound ones.

And now you're old-fashioned because you don't understand a computer? You never understood a gasoline engine. Or steam. Or an eletcric light bulb. Or an adding machine. Or an automatic gearshift. Or why an airplane flies. You never had to. And you don't now. You adapt, and have always adapted, to these technological advances. And you learn how to use them . . . to make them serve you.

Somebody always has to have the degrees from the universities in order to invent, to build, and to operate the new wonders. But most of the people always just use them, hiring others to keep them in working order. If the presidents of General Motors, Ford, and Chrysler were out driving on a country road in their Cadillac, Lincoln, and Imperial, and the engine went dead, would they know how to fix it? They might not even know how to open the hood. So they were old-fashioned?

By the sixties you are probably old-fashioned in some ways. You resist change from the ways you have done things. But for the young whippersnappers to say you are old-fashioned because you don't understand their new gadgets is a libel. You don't have to understand them to live with them and utilize them.

You might also keep in mind that it's not just you they are libeling. The forty-five-year-olds are also very old-fashioned now. Very. Just ask any whippersnapper.

Some Facts of Life

Retirement, apparently, has come to stay. There are no signs anywhere that the idea will go away. There are very few chances for you to beat it. Some good companies have occasionally made special deals to keep an employee on after retirement day, and there may always be a special case here and there. But, in general, any employees in any company or institution with a pension plan will have to retire, usually in the sixties, when the pension plan calls for retirement.

This is not because the company or institution is heartless, or chooses to be arbitrary. It is because employee relations have become so complex it has no choice. The price you and your employer have paid for your pension, labor contracts, and the perils of setting precedents make it extremely difficult for the company to tamper with the date you are scheduled to retire. In many cases, it may interest you to know, a company wrings its hands over having to retire a certain employee on a certain date. It sorely needs him for his or her value against a competitor. Or it wants him to stay because there is nobody in sight who can do his or her job so well. Or it dreads the fight that will develop for his or her job once retirement comes. But it dares not tamper with the system that has been set up.

There are increasing signs that the retirement age, which has usually been sixty-five for men and sixty-two for women, will soon drop to age sixty for both, and eventually to fifty-five. These no doubt will be voluntary retirement ages, with the "compulsory" ages remaining about where they are. But the inducements to retire early will be so strong that fewer and fewer people will want to push matters to the "compulsory" limit.

You who are retiring at this point in history are, in large measure, the retirement pioneers. Your own parents hardly got in on the Social Security benefits, and few of them ever heard of pensions and Medicare. Your children, on the other hand, are moving into a retirement banquet. Your generation is the historic link.

Another hard fact of retirement life is that while you are working, you are to most people a "what" and not a "who." You are the manager of this or that; you are a foreman; you are a sales representative of so-and-so; or you are a technician. This is how you are introduced to other people, and the Bill Smith or the Suzy Jones are only incidental to the what-you-are. On retirement you switch from a "what" to a "who." You have to fall back on your own personality for your image, your importance. And you may find that it hurts. Face up to this fact now, understand that it is something that must be, and then don't cry. You can expand your personality to compensate for the loss of the "what" that you were. Just do it.

And don't cry, don't think nobody loves you anymore, when, after retirement comes, your old company or institution and the old friends you had there begin fading into the distance. Both the employer and the employees have a business to get along with. Both are absorbed up to their eyebrows with it. They remember you. They love you still. They're just busy. As you were when the old-timers came back to make a call on you. Remember?

Another hard fact of retirement life is that when you retire you are being displaced, replaced, substituted for, done without —however you want to put it. You are out. The company can get along without you. And your successor in your job doesn't really want you to hang around and tell him how to do it. He'd rather you'd just go away and let him make his own mistakes. This is a bitter lash for the normal, vain human being. Again, don't cry. Better men than you have gone through it.

And finally comes the matter of your status in society, once you are retired. You are automatically regarded as a member of the old-folks set. If you are fifty-five or seventy it doesn't matter much. You are retired and therefore you're different. You are somewhat like the young lady who returns from her honeymoon after her wedding—she is now a nonvirgin, presumably.

You are now nonemployable, it is assumed. And people place you in a special segment of society.

It is these hard facts of retirement life—not so much in the money, the housing, and other mechanics—that are probably the fundamental causes of any worry you have about the future. Even though you won't admit it even to yourself, it is probably your concern over loss of status as it is wrapped up in these hard facts that bugs you most. Well, there's very little you can do to change them. You can squirm. You can worry from here to the grave. It is best that you accept the fact that they are bitter pills and that you'll have to swallow them. So swallow them. And get on with your life.

What has just been said will be about the only distasteful things said here. Not in order to be kind to you—you don't need kindness—but because they are about all there is to say in this vein. Everything else is based on your using a couple of the cells beneath that graying hair of yours—if you have any hair—to reason things out for yourself.

One of the important things for you to reason out is that, just maybe, somebody has been lying to you. Somebody who is about to retire, or already retired, and has a bigger mouth than you have.

Such stories as you've been hearing! Such plans! Such accomplishments! Such travels! Such fun! So much to do! Those you've heard talking must surely have the world by the tail, while you've got nothing planned but a little fishing off a lake pier on the second Tuesday after you retire and a trip with your wife to see an ill aunt twenty miles out of town.

All these other people surely must be brilliant. And you must be pretty dumb. And so you worry.

Well, all these other people—except possibly two of them—are telling you tales. They have to. Their pride is at stake. They very probably aren't planning, and haven't done, any more than you have in store—they haven't even motored out to see the ill aunt. But they aren't about to say so. They look better and they appear much more glamorous if they show themselves as busy and bubbling with fun. They know this—it's elemental psychology. And they play the game to the hilt. And send other people in the retirement class off biting their nails.

One of the funniest of retirement stories deals with this sort of thing. An industrial man and his wife had carefully hoarded their money for a trip to Europe following his retirement. They took it, then wound up in Naples, Italy, for a voyage back to New York.

Well, as any fool knows, this should be real glamour. The luxurious Italian liner, the blue Mediterranean, the swim decks, sumptuous food, galas. Then Gibraltar and the hucksters alongside in rowboats, and across the Atlantic.

This, they told their friends after returning, was as wonderful as it sounded. A year later they are still talking about the dream it all was.

But as a matter of fact the two of them thought they were going to die before they got to New York, first of seasickness (it was March and the sea was rough), then of boredom. Passengers of retirement age on the ship didn't see much fun at the galas where the young were whooping it up. They didn't want to be in the bars drinking from noon to 6 P.M. and from 11 P.M. until 3 A.M. And the bountiful meals, after two days, with no exercise and little else to divert them, became an ordeal instead of a pleasure. Shuffleboard? Well, not really. Walks around the deck? All you see is the same sea. And after Gibraltar it was too cold to swim or enjoy the open deck.

Eight days of this. And while they'll sing a song of it for the next five years, they wouldn't go on another ship voyage unless they were dragged aboard in chains.

So you've got to be wary of retired people bearing wonderful tales. Of travels, of California and Florida, of being very, very busy, of having a joyous time. You, no less than they, will be inclined to paint everything pretty. You'll see.

Some people, particularly men, can worry you by talking of their big prospects before they retire. An offer of a job here, another there. All sorts of invitations to join things, to assist with projects. They'll explain to you a whole panorama of delightful activities that lies before them.

This, generally, is what they called "whistling in the graveyard" when you were young. Don't let it worry you. Most of these people have no better prospects than you do.

Some Reassurance if You Need It

If there were ever a best time to be retiring, the men and women who are taking their pensions now have picked it. This third quarter of the twentieth century is when retirement is being discovered.

Since about the early 1950's new ideas about retirement and new proposals to make it better have been tumbling over each other. In the federal government, in business and institutions, in medicine, in housing, in finances, and in insurance, the 1950's and particularly the 1960's have been the Age of the Gray Hairs. Government has been involved in some of its greatest controversies over assistance to older people, granting that the birth of Social Security in the 1930's was a slight fuss, too. Business firms have set up special offices to serve their retiring employees. Insurance firms have come up with all kinds of insurance appealing directly to the retirement years. Investment houses have started offering special packages for retirement savings.

Builders have launched huge housing developments appealing exclusively to the retired. Hospitals have expanded to handle the older patients that new types of insurance and government programs are sending them. States and cities all over the land have started appealing to pensioners to move in to make their homes. Florida, among other states, has enacted tax laws that particularly favor older people.

In brief, you who are retiring now are fashionable. You are popular kids. Almost across the board society is seeking ways to make your life better.

You have become a major political factor to be reckoned with. Not just because there are about 20 million of you, but because most of you have children. Children, up until now, have borne the burden of their aging parents, taking them into their homes, providing care and necessities. For every proposal to make life better for retired people, through pensions, government aid, or however, there is not only your vote but the vote of your

209

children, too. It was the political support of children, many believe, that brought about medical aid under Social Security.

You may think you can't eat this new attention retired people have won, but as a matter of fact you can, in increased government aid and Social Security. But more important to you perhaps, and of more reassurance for the future, is that retired folks aren't just old folks anymore.

The Armor You Carry

The supply of bodyguards to accompany you into retirement is a little short this season. And nobody has any bows and arrows for you. So the armor you carry with you to ward off what fears or worries may beset you must come from somewhere else. And it must be of a different kind.

It must be something better than people standing on the sidelines as you retire and yelling, "Aw, don't be scared. Go on—jump!"

If it is to conquer your apprehensions, the armor must be your own mind. And the faith your mind can bring you.

Down on the Outer Banks, on the North Carolina coast, is a town called Nag's Head. It's a famous old vacation town. It has a pier. People from all over go there in summer to fish. Not long ago a man who had just retired from an industrial job in Connecticut was there, sitting alone at the far end of the pier and casting leisurely for whatever wanted to bite.

He had some interesting thoughts about retirement armor:

"I guess I had the same sort of worries about retiring that most people have," he said. "In fact, the prospects of it scared the daylights out of me when I passed my sixty-fourth birthday.

"I liked my job and my company. I didn't want to retire. I didn't want what looked to me to be the insecurity of a retirement income and no business connection. But I forced myself to stop thinking about the negative factors and to start looking for what must surely be some positive ones.

"The first one I found, and the only one I have needed since, was that my retirement was going to give me the only pure freedom I had had in all my lifetime. When I got my first job in my twenties I had wanted it in Southern California. But I got it in Dayton, Ohio, because I couldn't afford to go to California and didn't know I could get a job if I did.

"In the 1930's my plant closed down, and by now I had a wife and a child to support. I had no freedom to choose a job—I had to get anything I could. I made a connection in Pennsylvania. I didn't want to live in Pennsylvania. But it was a job.

"I held on for five years. Two more children arrived. Then came an opening for a job in Connecticut, with the company I was to remain with for over thirty years and finally retire from. But I wanted to go to Southern California. I wasn't free to go, not if I had any common sense. Connecticut offered a good job, good pay, and long-time security. I sized up my shaky financial status, took a look at my wife and three babies, and went to Connecticut.

"And what, with a job that now promised a lifetime career, did I do? I began to mold my thinking, my habits, my whole life, into the pattern of my company. Employees, if they are good ones, automatically do this. The pattern of my company was a good one. There was nothing wrong and nothing evil in what it thought and did. Still it was the company's pattern of life, not mine. Whatever sovereignty, whatever nobility, whatever imagination, I had were channeled into the company pattern. I have no argument with that. I want only to point out that if a man must work for a living, as most of us must, he must conform. He hasn't the freedom to be an oddball.

"With retirement he gets that freedom. And from the day when he wore diapers he hasn't had it.

"Now a man at retirement time doesn't want to be an oddball. But that sovereignty of mind, that nobility, that imagination, that all these working years have been confined are let loose. There are no inhibitions any longer.

"So what, out of a man's magnificent mind and spirit, can emerge in a climate of pure freedom?

"I puzzled over that for a long time. It occurred to me that a man who had been building Fords for twenty years might have

211

been a genius building Chevrolets. Or vice versa. That a man who had spent his career in the telephone business might have been a miracle man in radio. That a refinery man or a steel man might have been a musician, or a writer, or a painter.

"But how could he? There were the wife and three babies. The mortgage. The strong realization that a man, to be a man, had to get a job, be stable, and progress in normal channels.

"It's not a bad system. And I don't criticize it. But I came to the conclusion that under the system I could not possibly know —nor could anybody else—what greatness there might be inside me. Maybe I am the finest coal miner ever born. Who could say no? Maybe I am a novelist, a painter, an electronics wizard, a merchant prince in disguise. Maybe I am a brilliant trial lawyer, a poet, a master of politics. Maybe I am a genius at anything in the broad scope of human endeavor.

"Only with retirement—the first pure freedom a person ever has if he or she has a pension and Social Security—can one find out.

"So, I am in the process of finding out. I have allotted myself six months to untie the package that is me and to find out what's inside. I do my thinking while I fish, while I walk along the beach, as I sit on my porch back home watching the clouds, as I walk in the woods, as I listen to music.

"I am going to find out what spark of greatness may lie inside me. At the end of six months I will set out to fan it into a mission.

"From the time I got this idea that I might be wonderful at something—and who's to say I can't be?—I have had no worries about my retirement."

Again, your armor in retirement—your counterattack against what worries you have—lies in your own mind. Think a little on the facts of life. Try it. It won't hurt.

A Promotion That Is Yours

If what has been said so far has not opened a door through which you can conquer your worries about retiring, then maybe you had better get your worrying set up on a good professional basis. There are several ways to do this.

You can worry in front of your wife or husband and spend a good part of the day complaining how really tough life is. This will transplant your worry to the one who probably loves you most, and make him or her miserable, too.

You can worry in a rocker out on the front porch. This is very good because it enables the neighbors to say that you've turned into a despondent old grouch; and it invites the children to make fun of you.

You can worry in the presence of your friends. This is effective. It will drive all your friends away from you.

If you'll just worry enough in front of everybody, you can hit the jackpot because sooner or later somebody will mention the word "psychiatrist" and you may be lucky enough to wind up doing your worries in a "worry institution."

But before you get off on this kick, take one other matter under advisement: When you retire, you have a chance to gain the easiest and most important promotion you have ever had in your life. To get it you have to either move to a new town, or else outlive most people in your neighborhood who knew you at the time of retirement.

The technique of getting the promotion is quite simple. You just stop talking so much. For example, if you have been a blue-collar worker all your life, you can move to a new town and become a white-collar man. That is, if it matters to you. And it may, because some towns reserve their better civic, social, and religious positions for white collars. Of course, apart from not talking too much, you'll have to have a little savvy when you do talk. If you have been the custodian of the washrooms for your employer, you can retire to a new town as a sanitary engineer; you actually can, and people are doing it, because you were in fact a type of sanitary engineer.

You can retire as a minor cog in a large corporation and move to a new town as an executive. You don't have to say you were general manager, a hired hand, or a vice-president. You don't ʼave to lie. You can just say casually you were in a supervisory job, which you probably were, since even if you were a janitor you supervised the brooms.

A peculiar factor of human nature is involved here. The natives of any new town where you move will prefer to think you are an important person. They would rather meet an important person than an unimportant one, would rather introduce an important person to their friends. So what you do is not to lie but not to talk too much, and let nature take its course . . . and its course will be to promote you.

A peculiar factor of retirement is involved here, too. When you move into a new town as a retired person, nobody really cares very much what you were or what you did. Most people, in fact, will be bored if you try to tell them. They will accept you at face value, and promote you if they can. Unless, of course, you get locked up in jail.

So go on and move to your California town, be gracious, a good citizen, and let somebody introduce you as a VIP. You can't eat it, but it will get you invitations to some nice parties.

SOURCES OF ADDITIONAL MATERIAL

CHAPTER ONE

How to Retire and Enjoy It by Ray Giles, 1959; Fawcett Publications, Greenwich, Conn.

Look Forward to Your Retirement; U.S. Chamber of Commerce, Washington, D.C.

Preparation for Retirement in the Federal Government, edited by William L. Mitchell, 1968; American Association of Retired Persons, Washington, D.C.

Retirement and the Individual; hearings before the U.S. Senate Committee on Aging, 1967; U.S. Government Printing Office, Washington, D.C.

Social Security Benefits: What you earn and when, how much credit you need, Document No. 1404, 1968; Government Printing Office, Washington, D.C.

NOTE: Your public library will have books on all phases of retirement. Many of these books, you will find, are concerned with retirement programs as employers and organizations might set them up rather than with your personal needs. Your finest sources of personal material will be your own employer, your employer's pension company, and the lobby of any Social Security office.

CHAPTER TWO

Family Money Problems by Sidney Margolis; pamphlet No. 412; Public Affairs Committee, New York.

Retired Couple's Budget for Moderate Living Standard; Document No. 11132, 1969; Government Printing Office, Washington, D.C.

Retirement Income and Credit, Document No. 5018, 1967, and also *Tax Benefits for Older Americans*, Document No. 5569, 1967; Internal Revenue Service, Washington, D.C.

Trusts, wills, and professional money management—Most large banks and their branches have free booklets on these subjects. Go ask for them. In the public libraries you will find books on the subjects, but these are usually national in scope. Since wills and often trusts are governed by State laws, the banks will be your best source.

Your Retirement: Your Financial Resources and How You Might Use Them, 1962, Institute of Life Insurance, New York.

NOTE: The Welfare Office in your county can usually supply you with a low-income budget. Any bank or Savings & Loan will give you details on its various savings plans and what they pay. Stock brokerage houses will give you charts and pamphlets on what various investments produce. The company carrying your life insurance policies will give you data on annuities and other investment plans it has for retired people.

CHAPTER THREE

Florida Tax Facts, a booklet; Broward National Bank, Ft. Lauderdale, Fla.

Foreign Retirement Edens by Martha Logal Smith, 1969; Naylor Co., San Antonio.

How to Live in California by Phillip A. Ault, 1961; Dodd, Mead, New York.

Mobile Home and Travel Trailer Park Directory by R.A. Woodall; Woodall Publishing Co., Chicago.

Tax Facts for Older Americans, a chart comparing taxes in all the states; American Association of Retired Persons, Washington, D.C.

Where to Retire on a Small Income by Norman D. Ford, 1964; Harian Publications, Greenlawn, N.Y.

NOTE: Most state governments have travel and promotion departments that will supply you information about a given state. The Office of Governor can direct you to these departments. Almost any city of your choice will have a Chamber of Commerce that will give you booklets. Foreign embassies in Washington, D.C. or foreign consulates in the larger cities will give you information on foreign countries. Local newspapers in the town you like will tell you, largely through its want ads, what the town is.

CHAPTER FOUR

Conventional homes and apartments—See real estate agents in the town you choose.

Mobile homes—Write Mobile Homes Manufacturers Assn., 20 North Wacker Dr., Chicago, Ill., 60606, for details on the homes and where to park them.

Retirement homes—Ask your local pastor, as many of the better homes are operated by religious groups; or ask your labor union or your fraternal order, as they, too, have exceptional homes.

Retirement villages—Ask the Chamber of Commerce, a bank, or a real estate agent in the area. Most of these projects are commercial operations.

Others—Many cities are now getting low-rent housing projects, subsidized by government. Some are especially for the older people; all are usually operated in connection with the city government. See the local Housing Authority or ask at the office of the Mayor.

CHAPTER FIVE

A Brighter Later Life by Howard Whitman, 1961; Prentice-Hall, Englewood Cliffs, N.J.

Senior Forum by Beulah Collins, 1964; Fleet Publishing Corp., New York.

Social and Psychological Aspects of Aging by Clark Tibbitts and Wilma Donahue, 1962; Columbia University Press.

Handbook of Life Insurance, 1966; Institute of Life Insurance, New York.

NOTE: Almost any retirement booklet a husband picks up has references to the happiness and security of his wife. Almost all of the half-dozen or so Social Security and Medicare booklets available at a Social Security office have information pertinent to her. A husband, after reading the material himself, might gather it together on a special shelf at home for her to keep.

CHAPTER SIX

Now That You Are Retiring, 1963; Government Printing Office, Washington, D.C.

When Your Husband Retires by Mollie Hart, 1960; Appleton-Century-Crofts.

NOTE: A wife, if she can manage it, should get from her husband's employer a copy of all retirement information given to him, including data on his pension and fringe benefits. It will enable her to keep him straight on the parts of it he never read and reassure him when he decides he is being cheated.

CHAPTER SEVEN

Are You Planning on Living the Rest of Your Life? by Ralph H. Pollak and Arthur F. Strohmer Jr., 1965; Administration on Aging Publication No. 803; Government Printing Office, Washington, D.C.

Better Health After Fifty, 1964; Retirement Council; American Heritage Publishing Co., New York.

Food Guide for Older Folks, 1959; U.S. Dept. of Agriculture Bulletin No. 17; Government Printing Office, Washington, D.C.

More Life for Your Years; Committee on Aging; American Medical Assn., Chicago, Ill.

A wide variety of booklets and pamphlets on health from any county and state Medical Association, and from the Public Health Service, Washington, D.C.

SOURCES OF ADDITIONAL MATERIAL

CHAPTER EIGHT

Your Medicare Handbook, complete and authoritative data on what Medicare will and won't do; U.S. Dept. of Health, Education, and Welfare, Washington, D.C.; get free copy at any local Social Security office.

Medicaid, the joint federal-state program for the needy; operated by the states, all of which have different regulations; get details from county or State Welfare Department.

CHAPTER NINE

Legal Aspects of Planning by John A. Overholt, 1966; National Assn. of Retired Civil Employees, Washington, D.C.

Pre-Retirement Workshop, 1965; Bureau of Business Practice, Waterford, Conn.

You, the Law, and Retirement by Virginia Lehmann, 1965; Administration on Aging pamphlet; Government Printing Office, Washington, D.C.

NOTE: Most cities and almost all counties and states have Bar Associations. Some of them have booklets. However their main purpose is to refer a person to an attorney dealing with the particular problem involved.

CHAPTER TEN

Aging and Leisure by Robert W. Kleemeier (editor), 1961; Oxford University Press, New York.

New Directions, by U.S. State Department for retiring employees, 1966; Government Printing Office, Washington, D.C.

Older Workers in the Peace Corps, recruiting pamphlet; Peace Corps, Washington, D.C., 20525.

101 Ways to Enjoy Leisure, by Retirement Council, 1964; American Heritage Publishing Co., New York.

NOTE: All across the country adult schooling is available to retired people—in high schools, community colleges, and universities. Classes vary from crafts and job training to such things as political science and history. Inquire at the admissions office at any nearby school. If you find nothing that suits you, call at the office of any welfare organization in your community. All of them need volunteers. The schools and organizations in themselves offer substantial ways to use leisure, but both offer the significant fringe benefit of association with other retired people.

CHAPTER ELEVEN

Employment After Retirement, 1968; Document No. 8306; Government Printing Office, Washington, D.C.

Increasing Your Retirement and Other Income by Norman D. Ford, 1963; Harian Publications, Greenlawn, N.Y.

Operating a Small Business, Small Business Administration, Washington, D.C., 20416.

Help-wanted ads in the classified section of any metropolitan newspaper.

The official Employment Office of your state government, with headquarters usually in the State capital and branch offices over the State. Ask your state legislator or the County Courthouse for an address.

CHAPTER TWELVE

Best Places to Live When You Retire by Helen Heusinkveld and Noverre Musson, 1968; Frederick Fell, New York.

How to Prove Your Correct Age, most often needed by single men and women; write to Personal Census Service Branch, Bureau of the Census, Pittsburg, Kansas.

Job Training Opportunities for Older Women; Women's Bureau of U.S. Department of Labor, Washington, D.C.

National Directory of Housing for Older People, 1967; National Council on Aging, New York.

Your State Council on Aging; agencies funded by the Administration on Aging, Washington, D.C., and designed to enrich the lives of all older citizens. Ask your State legislator for address.

NOTE: The single man or woman who retires has a primary need for friends. These can be found easiest in community organizations. The Chamber of Commerce usually has a listing of them

CHAPTER THIRTEEN

Don't Retire from Life by Horace Greeley Smith, 1965; Rand McNally, Chicago.

Growing Old Gracefully by Paul H. Lorhan, 1967; Vantage Press, New York.

Let's Rejoin the Human Race by Joseph H. Peck, illustrated by Eric Gurney, 1962; Prentice-Hall, Englewood Cliffs, N.J.

"The Art of Retirement" by Michael T. Malloy, 1968; *National Observer*, Silver Springs, Md.

The New Guide to Happy Retirement by George W. Ware, 1968; Crown Publishers, New York.

NOTE: Write to the Superintendent of Documents, Government Printing Office, Washington, D.C., 20402, for free list of government publications available. These include activities and advice covering the whole field of retirement.

Magazines on Retirement

Aging; U.S. Department of Health, Education, and Welfare, Washington, D.C.

Dynamic Maturity; American Association of Retired Persons, Ojai, Calif.

Harvest Years; 104 East 40th Street, New York, N.Y.

Organizations on Retirement

American Association of Retired Persons, 1225 Con..ecticut Avenue, Washington, D.C., 20036.

Association of Retired Civil Employees; 1909 Q Street, Washington, D.C., 20009.

National Council on Aging; 315 Park Avenue South, New York, N.Y., 10010.